DO NOT OPEN THIS MATH BOOK!

Danica McKellar

Illustrations by

Maranda Maberry

WHAT?! YOU OPENED THE BOOK?! WHATEVER YOU DO, DON'T TURN ANY MORE PAGES, OKAY?

Crown Books for Young Readers ♛ New York

To my little boy Draco, whose impish charm inspired the best parts of Mr. Mouse!
I cherish introducing you to math concepts like the ones in this book
through homeschooling. I love you so much!

All rights reserved. Published in the United States by Crown Books for Young Readers,
an imprint of Random House Children's Books, a division of Penguin Random House LLC, New York.

Crown and the colophon are registered trademarks of Penguin Random House LLC.

Visit us on the Web! rhcbooks.com

Educators and librarians, for a variety of teaching tools, visit us at RHTeachersLibrarians.com

Library of Congress Cataloging-in-Publication Data
Names: McKellar, Danica, author. | Maberry, Maranda, illustrator.
Title: Do not open this math book! / Danica McKellar, illustrated by Maranda Maberry.
Description: First edition. | New York : Crown Books for Young Readers, [2018] | Audience: Ages 6–9. | Audience: K to grade 3. | Includes index.
Identifiers: LCCN 2017053345 | ISBN 978-1-101-93398-5 (flexibound) | ISBN 978-1-101-93399-2 (glb) | ISBN 978-1-101-93400-5 (epub)
Subjects: LCSH: Mathematics—Juvenile literature. | Arithmetic—Juvenile literature. | Math anxiety—Juvenile literature.
Classification: LCC QA11.2 .M42245 2018 | DDC 513—dc23

MANUFACTURED IN CHINA
10 9 8 7 6 5 4 3 2 1
First Edition

Introduction

What's Inside This OPEN Book, Hmm?

Chapter 3. Yummy Muffins and Buns!

Chapter 4. Buns, Not Butts!

Chapter 5. Strike a Pose!

Chapter 6. Filling Tins and Silly Grins:
Moving Numbers with Your Mind

Chapter 7. Imaginary Friends:
Tricks to Make Addition Easier!

Chapter 8. Stretch, Kitty, Stretch!
Using Expanded Form for Addition and Subtraction

What's with the "New Math," Anyway? . . .

As kids, many of us learned addition and subtraction with drills. We weren't taught much "method," so we came up with our own ways of thinking about it. Some of us would look at 9 + 5 and first change it to 10 + 4 in our heads, some of us would count on our fingers, and some of us would simply memorize that 9 + 5 = 14. As it turns out, if we change 9 + 5 to 10 + 4, we're thinking more about the *nuts and bolts* of what's going on, which is at the heart of the methods being taught in the "new math" today.

I mean, there's nothing wrong with the idea of a nuts-and-bolts approach, but these days, even first- and second-grade math homework often looks overly complicated, even unrecognizable at times—especially to parents! Why? Partly because many of the new methods try to re-create subtle thought processes on paper for what could be very simple problems. Often, kids are even asked to *think* about problems in a certain way—which may or may not match up with your child's way of thinking.

Is there value in enriching our children's understanding of these basic math skills beyond pure memorization? Of course! But there is a danger in making things too complicated, and we must remember that every child learns differently. . . .

In this book, I bridge the gap between the straightforward techniques we learned in school and the more involved methods being taught today. Mixed in with the kid-friendly humor and silliness, this book decodes new math techniques and brings the new methods into easy, fun, and familiar territory—with a bonus that your kids' math homework won't look so foreign to you in the future! Sometimes it's as simple as translating new words—for example, in subtraction, instead of "borrowing," today's term is "ungrouping." I'll also explain how to work with the newer tools like ten frames, number bonds, fact families, and more, in plain (and fun!) language that we can all relate to. When it comes to adding and subtracting, students will be empowered to choose which method to use, or no "method" at all.

So here's to giving our kids a solid understanding of the basics of addition and subtraction (and number sense!) to prepare them for *math success* in elementary school, high school, and beyond—whether the new methods are just fads or are here to stay.

Congratulations . . . and have fun reading this book with your child!

PS: While some advanced readers might enjoy this book alone, most children will benefit from an adult reading it to them—an adult who just might have a lot of fun with the antics of Mr. Mouse.

Throughout the book are "Game Time" sections with practice problems for your child. You'll notice that I didn't leave room in the book for you to do the math, so you'll want to have a separate piece of paper handy. This was a deliberate choice to keep the book pages clean so your child can do the problem sets more than once for better mastery of the material. As an added bonus, siblings or friends will be able to use the book as well. Enjoy!

Chapter 1

Stinky Toes and Hopping Frogs:
Making 10 in Different Ways

Making 10 . . . with Fingers!

Hold up your 10 fingers (or toes!). Now count them to make sure they're all there. Did any run away? No? That's a relief! Close your fingers together, and try moving just your right pinkie finger to the side, to create 9 + 1.

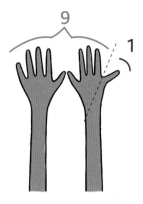

And since there are a total of 10 fingers on your hands, we can see how 9 + 1 = 10! Now try moving your right ring finger to meet your right pinkie, to show how 8 + 2 = 10.

There are lots of ways to make 10, and they can ALL be done on your fingers!

Ways to Make 10!

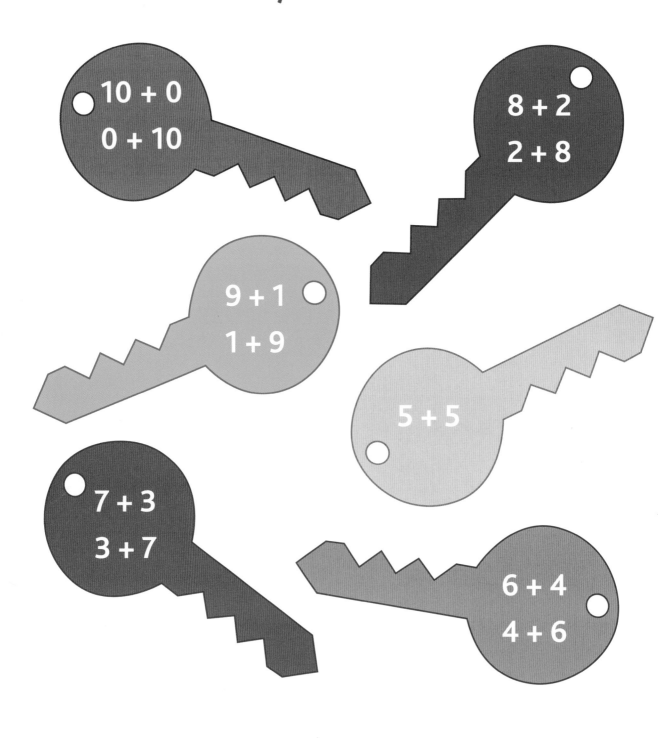

GAME TIME!

Can you figure out which math sentence goes with each set of hands?

I'll do the first one for you!

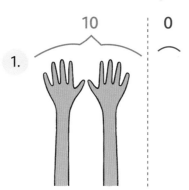

1.

Let's Play: I see all 10 fingers on the left and no fingers on the right. Which math sentence does this show? Yep, 10 + 0 = 10!

Answer: 10 + 0 = 10

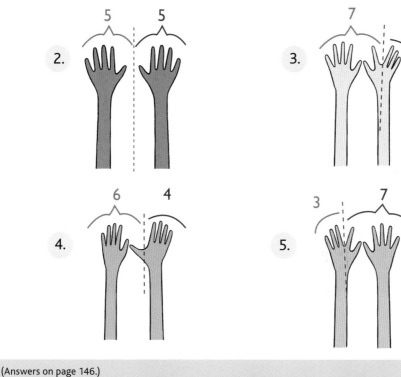

2.

3.

4.

5.

(Answers on page 146.)

A New Puppy! Making 10 on the Stairs

Pretend you just got a new puppy, but she ran up 10 steps and now you have to go get her. You're really excited, so you want to run, but you're also really tired because you've been playing sports all day!

You run up the first 6 steps, but then you get too tired and so you have to walk up the last 4 steps. You still make it up the full 10 steps, right? Here's the math sentence for how you get up the 10 steps:

$$6 + 4 = 10$$
$$(\text{run}) + (\text{walk}) = (\text{total})$$

But maybe you're REALLY tired, so you only run up the first 3 steps and walk up the rest of the way. Here's a math sentence for that:

$$3 + 7 = 10$$
$$(\text{run}) + (\text{walk}) = (\text{total})$$

No matter how tired you are, you're definitely going to come up with some combination of running and walking to make 10 total. I mean, it's your new puppy!

GAME TIME!

Answer the questions about going up 10 steps, and look at the stairs below for help. I'll do the first one for you!

1. You *ran* up 8 steps, you're going to *walk* up the rest, and there are 10 steps total. How many steps did you have to *walk* up? Then write the math sentence on a piece of paper.

Let's Play: If there is a total of 10 steps and we run up 8, then we'd be right at the little 8 on the stairs. See it? Then we can count 2 more steps, and that gets us to the top, to 10! And we can write this math sentence as 8 + 2 = 10. Done!
Answer: We'd walk up 2 steps. 8 + 2 = 10

2. You *ran* up 3 steps, you're going to *walk* up the rest, and there are 10 steps total. How many steps did you have to *walk* up? Then write the math sentence.

3. You *ran* up 9 steps, you're going to *walk* up the rest, and there are 10 steps total. How many steps did you have to *walk* up? Then write the math sentence.

4. You *ran* up 5 steps, you're going to *walk* up the rest, and there are 10 steps total. How many steps did you have to *walk* up? Then write the math sentence.

5. You *ran* up 7 steps, you're going to *walk* up the rest, and there are 10 steps total. How many steps did you have to *walk* up? Then write the math sentence.

(Answers on page 146.)

Hopping Frogs: 10 on the Number Line!

Another way to make 10 is on a **number line**. Number lines might remind you of our numbered stairs on page 16! Number lines are great, especially when frogs are hopping on them.

A **number line** is a line with numbers placed in their correct position. Notice that on a number line, numbers get *bigger* as we go to the right, and *smaller* as we go to the left.

LARGER ⟶

⟵ SMALLER

0 1 2 3 4 5 6 7 8 9 10 11 12

We can use number lines to help us add and subtract! If we want to *add* numbers, we hop to the *right,* and if we want to *subtract* (or take away), we hop to the *left*!

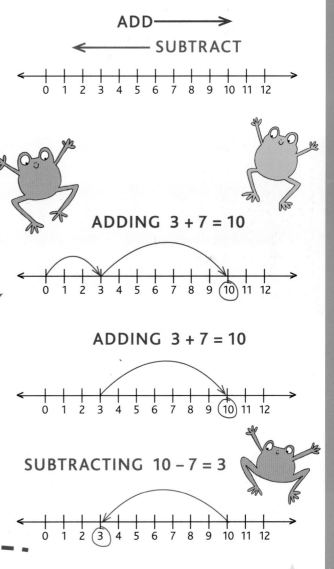

ADD ⟶

⟵ SUBTRACT

0 1 2 3 4 5 6 7 8 9 10 11 12

Let's make 10 on the number line like this: 3 + 7 = 10. We'll pretend there's a frog on the 0 and she hops to the 3, since that's the number we are starting with. Then, to add 7, she just hops 7 spots to the right! And that lands her on the 10.

ADDING 3 + 7 = 10

0 1 2 3 4 5 6 7 8 9 (10) 11 12

For 3 + 7 = 10, we could also have the frog *start* on the 3, and then hop 7 spots to the right. Either way, we land on the 10!

ADDING 3 + 7 = 10

0 1 2 3 4 5 6 7 8 9 (10) 11 12

What if we wanted to do the subtraction problem 10 − 7 = 3? Well, the frog would start on the 10, and then hop to the *left* 7 spots. That would land her on the 3. Try it yourself!

SUBTRACTING 10 − 7 = 3

0 1 2 (3) 4 5 6 7 8 9 10 11 12

See how it works? And, of course, we can add and subtract other numbers on the number line, too—it doesn't always have to just be about 10!

When adding numbers on the number line, some teachers will have you start at the first number, and some will want you to start hopping from zero. Both ways will give us the same answer—in this case, 5! Here are two ways it could look:

See how we can either start from the 2, or we can start back at 0 and hop to the 2? Both ways work, but the first way is *definitely* best for subtraction.

GAME TIME!

Use the number line to add and subtract the numbers below.

Hop, froggy, hop! I'll do the first one for you.

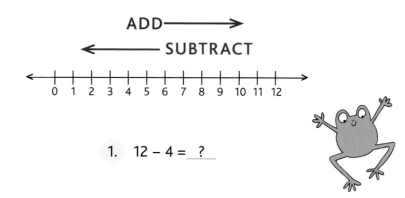

ADD ———————→

←——————— SUBTRACT

0 1 2 3 4 5 6 7 8 9 10 11 12

1.   12 – 4 = __?__

Let's Play: This means our frog starts on the 12, and if we're subtracting 4, we'd hop to the left 4 spots—because we want to get a smaller number, right? Let's hop!

12 – 4 = 8

0 1 2 3 4 5 6 7 (8) 9 10 11 12

And lookie there, we ended up at 8. And that's our answer!
12 - 4 = 8. Done!
Answer: 12 - 4 = 8

For the following exercises, you can either draw your own number lines, print some at DoNotOpenThisMathBook.com, or just use your finger to point on the number line on the next page and do it in your head!

Keep going! ——————→

2. $5 + 2 =$ ___?___   3. $11 - 1 =$ ___?___

4. $8 + 3 =$ ___?___   5. $8 - 3 =$ ___?___

6. $6 + 4 =$ ___?___   7. $10 - 3 =$ ___?___

ADD ⟶

⟵ SUBTRACT

PHEW! AFTER ALL THAT HOPPING, I GUESS WE NO LONGER HAVE TO WONDER HOW FROGS STAY IN SUCH GREAT SHAPE!

NOBODY WAS WONDERING THAT.

BUT I BET YOU WERE WONDERING HOW CUTE FROGS ARE WHEN THEY ARE BABIES, RIGHT?

SOMEBODY HELP ME.

(Answers on page 146.)

Tadpoles and Frogs: Ten Frames!

Let's get back to making 10! Did you know that baby frogs don't look anything like frogs? They're called tadpoles, and they look more like little fish!

Imagine if we had little tadpole houses, and slowly but surely, the tadpoles grew into frogs. So it starts out looking like this:

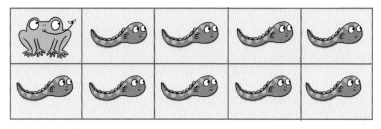

After several weeks of good food and good times, the tadpoles begin to become frogs! There are still 10 little creatures, but now we see 1 frog + 9 tadpoles. This is a way of showing how 1 + 9 = 10. See what I mean?

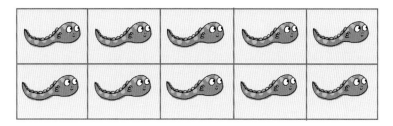

$$1 + 9 = 10$$

And below, we see 3 frogs and 7 tadpoles, which shows 3 + 7 = 10.

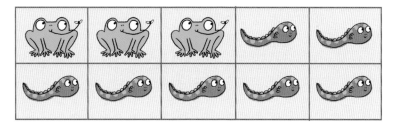

$$3 + 7 = 10$$

Write the math sentence that describes what is shown. I'll do the first one for you!

1.

Let's Play: We see 8 frogs and 2 tadpoles and there are 10 little creatures total, so the math sentence that describes this would be 8 + 2 = 10. Ta-da!

Answer: 8 + 2 = 10

2.

3.

4.

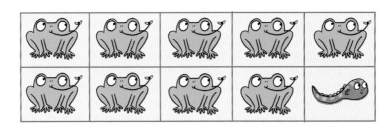

(Answers on page 146.)

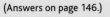
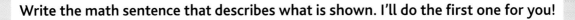

Upside-Down Alien Heads?
Hungry Guys? Number Bonds!

Number bonds are cute little drawings that have two smaller numbers in circles that add up to the bigger number in a rectangle. The number bonds below show us three different math sentences. See what I mean?

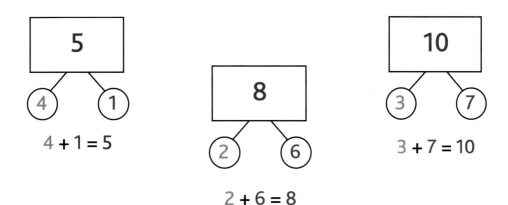

What do number bonds look like to you? Maybe upside-down alien heads?

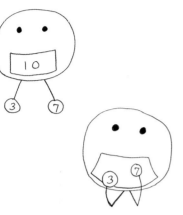

Or instead, maybe rectangular mouths with little arms coming out from them? Let's draw a head around that mouth, and if those little arms had elbows, then I suppose they could bend, putting the smaller numbers into the mouth, where the two numbers would be smashed together and create the bigger number!

So once the 3 and the 7 get inside, they smoosh together and make 10. Whatever you like to imagine, these number bonds are something you might see in your math class—and they're another great way to practice all the different ways to make 10!

MAKING NUMBERS WITH 10 . . . TEENS!

Speaking of 10 . . . have you ever noticed anything interesting about the "teen" numbers? They are all 10 + the number they sound like!

10 + 3 = 13 Ten + three = thirteen

10 + 4 = 14 Ten + four = fourteen

10 + 5 = 15 Ten + five = fifteen

10 + 6 = 16 Ten + six = sixteen

10 + 7 = 17 Ten + seven = seventeen

10 + 8 = 18 Ten + eight = eighteen

10 + 9 = 19 Ten + nine = nineteen

See how each of the teen numbers has exactly 1 TEN in it? And gosh, TEEN looks just like TEN, but with an extra "E"!

THIS IS SO ANNOYING! WHY ARE THERE SO MANY DIFFERENT WAYS TO THINK ABOUT 10? I MEAN, TEN FRAMES, NUMBER LINES, CRAZY NUMBER-BOND *ALIEN* HEADS. . . .

AND THERE ARE EVEN MORE! WHEN I WAS A LITTLE GIRL, MY MOM USED TO HOLD 10 COLORED PENCILS BETWEEN HER TWO HANDS AND SHIFT ONE AT A TIME WHILE I SAID THE MATH SENTENCES OUT LOUD SO I'D LEARN THEM MORE EASILY!

One and nine, or two and eight,

Making ten is really great.

Three and seven, four and six,

Holding carrots, pencils, or sticks!

Five and five, zero and ten,

This is fun—let's do it again!

Stinky Toes and Hopping Frogs: Making 10 in Different Ways

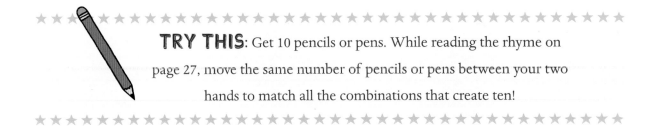

TRY THIS: Get 10 pencils or pens. While reading the rhyme on page 27, move the same number of pencils or pens between your two hands to match all the combinations that create ten!

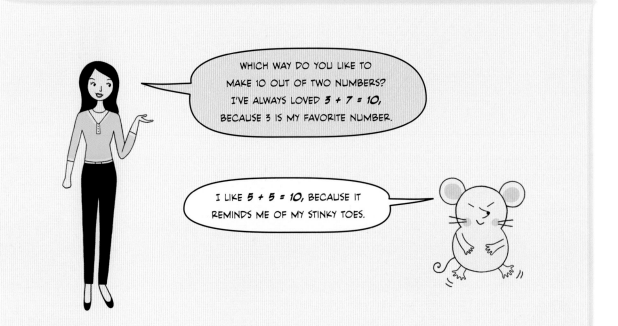

> WHICH WAY DO YOU LIKE TO MAKE 10 OUT OF TWO NUMBERS? I'VE ALWAYS LOVED *3 + 7 = 10,* BECAUSE 3 IS MY FAVORITE NUMBER.

> I LIKE *5 + 5 = 10,* BECAUSE IT REMINDS ME OF MY STINKY TOES.

What's YOUR favorite way to make 10?

Chapter 2

How to Destroy a Turkey Sandwich:

Fact Families

Yummy . . . Fact Families!

If you're like a lot of kids, then you prefer your sandwiches plain—no goopy mustard or anything else with a weird texture, thank you very much! Just plain bread and plain turkey, perhaps? Or ham? Or maybe you're a cheese-sandwich type, like Mr. Mouse? In any case, I'll use turkey for our example because it's my favorite and you can't stop me. (Just try.)

We'll add some turkey to some sliced bread, and lookie, we get a sandwich! Yep, that's a *fact*.

We could write this fact as a "sandwich sentence":

turkey   +   bread   =   sandwich

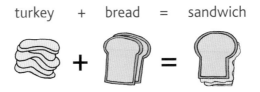

I guess we also could have written:

bread   +   turkey   =   sandwich

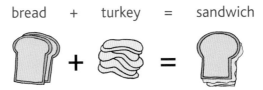

And that's another *fact*. Well, it's sort of the same fact—they're saying the same thing, after all!

Okay, but what if we wanted to *take apart* the sandwich? I mean, if we took the turkey off, would we still have a sandwich? Nope! We'd just be left with the bread.

sandwich   –   turkey   =   bread

See what we did there? We had a sandwich, then we took away (or subtracted) the turkey, and we ended up with bread! And that's another fact, isn't it? What if instead we started off with a sandwich and we took away the bread? What would we be left with? Yep! Just the turkey! That "sandwich sentence" looks like this:

sandwich   –   bread   =   turkey

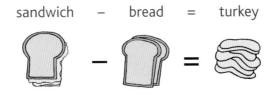

Yet another fact. We've now created four facts out of *the same three things*—all of these facts are *related* to each other. So we could call this a **fact family**, you see?

turkey + bread = sandwich	bread + turkey = sandwich
sandwich − turkey = bread	sandwich − bread = turkey

And we can make fact families out of math sentences, too!

??? WHAT'S IT CALLED? ???

A **fact family** for addition and subtraction is a group of addition and subtraction facts that all use the same numbers! For example:

4 + 5 = 9	5 + 4 = 9
9 − 5 = 4	9 − 4 = 5

The subtraction sentences start with the biggest number. Makes sense, right? We have to start with the whole sandwich before we can destroy it. Here's another fact family:

2 + 10 = 12	10 + 2 = 12
12 − 10 = 2	12 − 2 = 10

THIS CHAPTER IS OKAY.

And here's how this fact family would look in terms of sandwiches. Easy, right?

2 + 10 = 12

turkey — add bread — whole sandwich

12 − 10 = 2

Sandwich — take away bread — we're left with turkey

10 + 2 = 12

bread — add turkey — whole sandwich

12 − 2 = 10

Sandwich — take away turkey — we're left with bread

Lunch Boxes: Part-Part-Whole!

Can you imagine just carrying around your sandwich, apple, and water in your arms at school all day? A lunch box sure is a lot easier, right?

When it comes to fact families, a box can make things easier, too. . . .

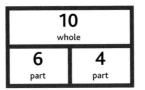

Some people call these **part-part-whole boxes,** since the two **parts** (of the sandwich) add up to the **whole** (sandwich). It still *means* the four math sentences—it's just a much shorter way to write it!

Many textbooks now say there are *eight* facts in a fact family, not four—all they are doing is rewriting the same four facts, but putting the answer in front. In this case, we'd include 10 = 6 + 4, 10 = 4 + 6, 4 = 10 − 6, and 6 = 10 − 4. Seems like a lot of extra writing to me, but do whatever your teachers ask you to do (or they might get mad at me)!

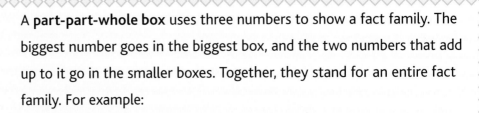

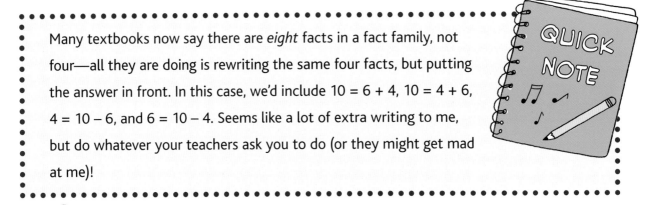

A **part-part-whole box** uses three numbers to show a fact family. The biggest number goes in the biggest box, and the two numbers that add up to it go in the smaller boxes. Together, they stand for an entire fact family. For example:

Sometimes the "whole" will be on top with the "parts" underneath, and sometimes the "whole" will be on the bottom with the "parts" on top. But the biggest number—the "whole"—will always be in the biggest box!

It's just two ways of writing the same thing!

IF THE "WHOLE" IS ON THE BOTTOM, WILL THE "PARTS" FALL OUT?

YOU THINK YOU'RE PRETTY FUNNY, DON'T YOU?

I HAVE MY MOMENTS.

In any case, it's all really just sandwiches. And remember, the biggest number is always the whole sandwich.

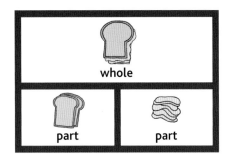

Write down the fact family for the given numbers: two addition sentences and two subtraction sentences. Remember the sandwiches if it helps. I'll do the first one for you!

1.

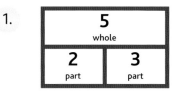

5
whole

2	**3**
part	part

Let's Play: Time to make some sandwiches! The biggest number is 5, so that's the whole sandwich, right? Then 2 and 3 are the bread and turkey. To build our sandwich, we could do **2 + 3 = 5**, or we could do **3 + 2 = 5**, right?

Now let's destroy the sandwich! That's **5 – 2 = 3**, or we could also destroy it like this: **5 – 3 = 2**. (I mean, we didn't have to use sandwiches, but I know Mr. Mouse appreciates it.) Done!

Answer: 2 + 3 = 5   3 + 2 = 5   5 – 2 = 3   5 – 3 = 2

2.

9	
whole	
1	**8**
part	part

3.

2	**8**
part	part
10	
whole	

4.

6	
whole	
3	**3**
part	part

5.

4	**3**
part	part
7	
whole	

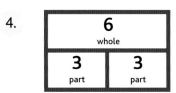

Now you'll figure out what goes in the missing spot (either the turkey, bread, or sandwich) and make your own part-part-whole box, with the new number filled in, too. I'll do the first one for you!

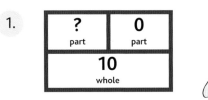

1.

?	0
part	part
10	
whole	

Let's Play: Hmm, the whole sandwich is 10. One part is "0", so what do we need to add to 0 so that we can make 10? We have to add the entire 10! So "10" goes in the missing spot. Done!

Answer: 10

10	0
10	

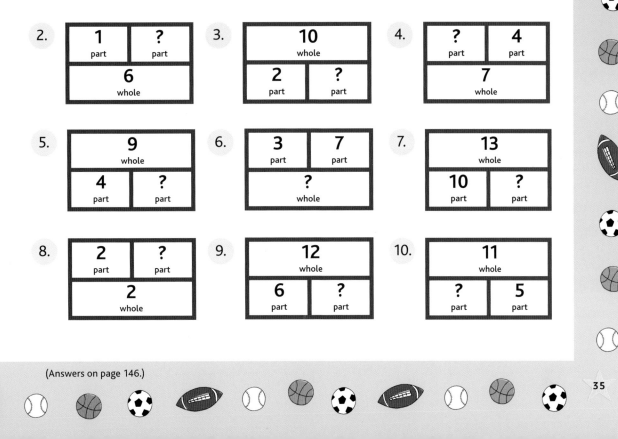

2.

1	?
part	part
6	
whole	

3.

10	
whole	
2	?
part	part

4.

?	4
part	part
7	
whole	

5.

9	
whole	
4	?
part	part

6.

3	7
part	part
?	
whole	

7.

13	
whole	
10	?
part	part

8.

2	?
part	part
2	
whole	

9.

12	
whole	
6	?
part	part

10.

11	
whole	
?	5
part	part

(Answers on page 146.)

Detective Work!
Find the Missing Number

Now we're going to figure out the missing numbers in these equations . . . like a detective!

WAIT, DID YOU SAY *EQUATIONS?* ISN'T THAT ALGEBRA, LIKE FOR OLDER KIDS?

SORT OF! IT'S LIKE THE VERY BEGINNING OF ALGEBRA. BUT YOU'LL SEE--WE'VE *ALREADY BEEN DOING IT.* NOW IT JUST LOOKS A LITTLE DIFFERENT. . . .

Instead of filling in an empty *box*, we'll be filling an empty spot in an equation—in other words, a math sentence like this:

$$4 + ? = 10$$

We can read this math sentence by using the word "what" where we see the question mark: "Four plus *what* equals ten?" Try saying that out loud!

And what's the answer? **6!** And the math sentence becomes 4 + **6** = 10. Nice! And instead of a question mark, we could use a flower or a car, or even a letter like x, y, or z! It doesn't matter what is in that spot—*our job is to figure out what number goes in that spot to make the math sentence true.*

DOING MATH IS FUN BECAUSE IT'S LIKE SOLVING A PUZZLE TO GET THE ANSWER.

Here's an example!

$$9 - \text{♥} = 4$$

We know the ♥ must be standing in for **5**, because that's the number that makes the math sentence true: $9 - \textbf{5} = 4$. See?

Here are some more:

$$4 + 2 = \text{🚗}$$

The 🚗 must be **6**, since $4 + 2 = \textbf{6}$.

$$\text{🌼} - 2 = 7$$

The 🌼 must be **9**, since $9 - 2 = 7$.

$$10 - ? = 3$$

The ? must be **7**, since $10 - \textbf{7} = 3$.

GAME TIME!

Just like we filled in the missing boxes on page 35, let's put on our thinking caps and figure out the missing numbers. I'll do the first one for you!

1. $11 - $ 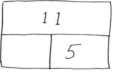 $ = 5$

Let's Play: Hmm . . . what is the cheese standing in for? Let's be detectives! First of all, is 11 the *whole* sandwich or just a *part*? It must be the whole sandwich, since something is going to be taken away from it, and then we'll end up with 5. See what I mean? You can also write it out like we did on page 35, if it helps:

1 1	
	5

So what do we have to add to 5 to get 11, the whole sandwich? That's 6, since 5 + 6 = 11. Yep, the missing part is 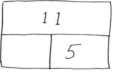 =6, and now we write the sentence: 11 – 6 = 5. Done!

Answer: 11 – 6 = 5

2. $2 + \underline{\ ?\ } = 5$

3. $8 + 3 = $ ♥

4. $9 - \underline{\ ?\ } = 4$

5. $7 - $ 🚗 $ = 4$

6. $\underline{\ ?\ } - 1 = 8$

7.   🌼 $ + 6 = 8$

8.   🚗 $ - 3 = 7$

9. $7 - \underline{\ ?\ } = 2$

10. $10 + $ 🧀 $ = 17$

(Answers on page 146.)

PUT YOUR THINKING CAP ON!

Maybe you noticed that on page 38 I said to put your thinking cap on. A "thinking cap" is an imaginary hat that helps a person to focus and get ready to solve problems! What would your thinking cap look like? If you want, you can get out a piece of paper and draw your own or even *make* your own—or you can just *imagine* what it might look like. Do you love football? Make your thinking cap a football helmet! Or how about a sparkly majestic crown, like a queen would wear to rule her country? Or maybe a pirate's hat? Or even a baseball cap with a lightsaber shooting off the front like a laser? Anything that makes you feel *powerful* can work!

Imagine putting your thinking cap on, and let yourself feel *really* smart, powerful, and ready to tackle any problem! Say to yourself, "I got this!"

Addition Chart!

Now that we understand how fact families work, let's take a look at a big table of addition facts!

Here's how it works: If we want to add two numbers together, like 5 + 6, we put one finger on the "5" on the top row, and with our other hand, we put a finger on the "6" on the left side. Then we slide our fingers toward the center until they meet—making sure to stay inside the correct row and column, of course! And in this case, our fingers meet at "11"! So 5 + 6 = 11.

Addition Chart

+	0	1	2	3	4	5	6	7	8	9	10
0	0	1	2	3	4	5	6	7	8	9	10
1	1	2	3	4	5	6	7	8	9	10	11
2	2	3	4	5	6	7	8	9	10	11	12
3	3	4	5	6	7	8	9	10	11	12	13
4	4	5	6	7	8	9	10	11	12	13	14
5	5	6	7	8	9	10	11	12	13	14	15
6	6	7	8	9	10	11	12	13	14	15	16
7	7	8	9	10	11	12	13	14	15	16	17
8	8	9	10	11	12	13	14	15	16	17	18
9	9	10	11	12	13	14	15	16	17	18	19
10	10	11	12	13	14	15	16	17	18	19	20

This can be a good reference, but even better than needing a chart is to be able to figure it out on our own, so here are some tricks to make addition easier!

SHORTCUT ALERT!

EASY TRICKS FOR LEARNING SOME OF THE FACTS

COUNTING ON

I SEE WHAT YOU DID THERE.

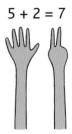

Here's a great trick you can count on: if we want to add anything plus a small number, we can just "count on" to find the answer. For example, 11 + 2 = ? We start with 11, and then "count on" 2 steps from 11: "12, 13." And that's our answer! 11 + 2 = 13. If the problem were 3 + 9, we'd still start with the bigger number, 9, and "count on" 3 steps from 9: "10, 11, 12." See?

FIVES

| 5 + 1 | 5 + 2 | 5 + 3 | 5 + 4 | 5 + 5 | 5 + 2 = 7 |

Whenever you add 5 plus a number between 1 and 5, it's really easy, because it's like our fingers! Just picture your hands (or use your hands), and you probably won't even have to count to know what the answer is!

Remember all that time we spent in Chapter 1 on "making 10"? There was a reason—it's really helpful to know all the ways to make 10! That way, if you have something like 4 + 7 = ?, you can think, "Hmm, I already know that 4 + 6 = 10, so I guess 4 + 7 = 11." After all, since 7 is 1 more than 6, the answer must be 1 more than 10!

DOUBLES

These are in the boxes on the purple diagonal of the big chart on page 39—it's all the facts where a number adds to itself! It's like the number is looking in the mirror. OMG, they're totally obsessed with themselves . . . well, they are famous, after all, and we should do our best to learn them!

Here they are!

1 + 1 = 2	2 + 2 = 4	3 + 3 = 6	4 + 4 = 8	5 + 5 = 10
6 + 6 = 12	7 + 7 = 14	8 + 8 = 16	9 + 9 = 18	10 + 10 = 20

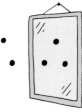

I'll show you some more tricks in Chapter 6 for the bigger facts like 6 + 6 = 12. We'll be filling muffin tins, and it's super fun and easy!

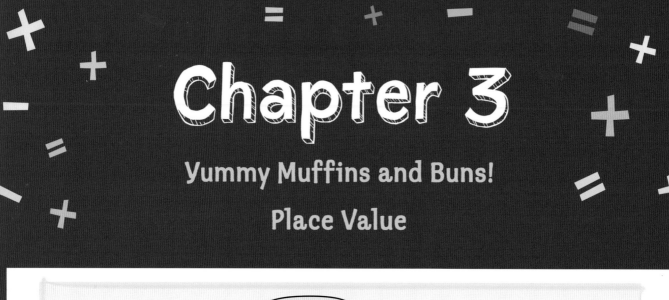

Chapter 3

Yummy Muffins and Buns!

Place Value

Introducing
Lin and Larry!

Tins and Toasty Buns: I'm Tired of Counting!

Once upon a time, a baker named Lin made hot toasty buns for people to eat. Her twin brother, Larry, helped, too!

Everybody loved the buns, so Lin made more and more! Larry would help people to their cars with all the buns they ordered, but often Larry had a hard time counting them and carrying them. He was so tired from all the counting, and he kept dropping them on the ground! Then they got a great idea to use *tins,* which really helped Larry. You see, *all the tins were the same size,* and they always held *10 buns each.* So instead of having to count 10 buns like this . . .

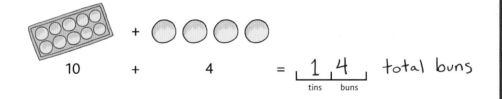

. . . they could instead fill up a tin, and—ta-da!—they knew for sure there were 10 buns inside, without even having to count. Wow!

So if someone ordered 14 buns, Lin could just fill up a tin, and then add 4 more, like this:

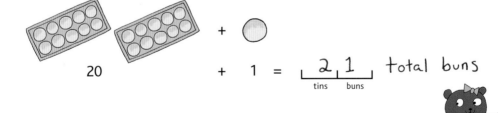

Or if someone ordered 21 buns, Lin would just give them 2 full tins and 1 extra bun, because:

Using tins is a GREAT way to keep track of how many buns we have, without all the trouble of counting every single bun.

"Each tin holds 10 buns," said Lin to Larry.
"Very easy to load and so easy to carry!
So turn that frown into a grin—
Whenever we can, let's <u>fill a tin</u>!"

When we see an equals sign, =, it means "equals," or "is the same as," so when we're reading it, we can think about those words in our heads! For example:

$$2 + 3 = 5$$

"Two plus three *is the same as* **five**."

"Two plus three equals **five**."

$$8 - 2 = 6$$

"Eight take away two *is the same as* **six**."

"Eight take away two equals **six**."

TWO PLUS THREE
IS THE SAME
AS FIVE.

$$3 \text{ tins} = 30 \text{ buns}$$

"Three tins *is the same as* thirty buns."

"Three tins equals thirty buns."

Notice that since there are 10 buns in each tin, we also know that:

2 tins *is the same as* **20 buns**

3 tins = 30 buns   4 tins = 40 buns

Can you see the pattern? How many buns are in 5 tins? Yep—50 buns!

Can you figure out the rest? Say them out loud!

6 tins = _?_ buns   8 tins = _?_ buns

7 tins = _?_ buns   9 tins = _?_ buns

GAME TIME!

Write the number of full tins and the number of extra buns.

Then write them together for the total! I'll do the first one for you.

1.

How many tins? How many extra buns? In other words, how many total

buns?   ?   ?
           tins   buns

Let's Play: Hmm, there are **4** tins, so that goes in the tins place, and there are **3** extra buns, so that goes in the buns place—and, yep, there are **43** total buns. That's a lot of buns! I'm so glad we didn't have to count them all!

Answer: 4 , 3 ,   43 total
          tins buns

2.   ?   ?
                                    tins   buns

How many tins? How many extra buns? So how many total buns?

3.   ?   ?
                                    tins   buns

How many tins? How many extra buns? So how many total buns?

4.   ?   ?
                                    tins   buns

How many tins? How many extra buns? So how many total buns?

(Answers on page 146.)

Place Value—Piece o' Cake!

Have you ever heard the word "value"? It means how big or important something is. So a really big piece of cake might have more *value* to you than a small piece of cake. And that piece of cake is going to have more *value* to you if it's on the table than if it's in the trash, right? (Don't go into the trash for it—yuck!) Sometimes the place *where* a thing is changes its value! And the same is true for numbers— it's called **place value**.

WHAT'S IT CALLED? ? ? ?

Place value is the *value* of a number like 0–9, depending on the *place* where it is!

For example, the *place value* of 5 in the number 54 is **50**, but the *place value* of 4 in the number 54 is just **4**.

54

means "50"   means "4"

You might have heard the term "place value" before. We just played a game on page 45 and learned that, for example, if the 3 is in the tins place, it stands for 30 buns. But if the 3 is in the buns place, it stands for 3 buns. So the value of the 3—how many buns it stands for—changes depending on where the 3 is. That's place value!

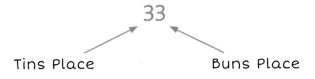

33

Tins Place   Buns Place

Numbers mean different things depending on where they are. That 3 on the left sure has more value than the 3 on the right, doesn't it?

GAME TIME!

Lin and Larry are back at it, making lots of buns and filling tins, and they need our help! If they write the total, can we figure out how many full tins they'll need and how many extra buns will be left over? Yes, we can! I'll do the first one for you!

1.   15 is _?_ tins and _?_ extra buns.

Let's Play: Well, looking at 15, we can see that there is a 1 in the tins place, so there must be 1 full tin and 5 leftover buns!
Answer: 1 tin and 5 extra buns

2.   24 is _?_ tins and _?_ extra buns.

3.   45 is _?_ tins and _?_ extra buns.

4.   84 is _?_ tins and _?_ extra buns.

5.   19 is _?_ tins and _?_ extra buns.

6.   37 is _?_ tins and _?_ extra buns.

7.   80 is _?_ tins and _?_ extra buns.

8.   61 is _?_ tins and _?_ extra buns.

9.   28 is _?_ tins and _?_ extra buns.

(Answers on page 146.)

Tins and Buns = Tens and Ones:
Return of the Ten Frames

Okay, now I'm going to tell you a secret: tins and buns are like tens and ones! Instead of a *tins* place, we have a *tens* place, and instead of a *buns* place, we have a *ones* place.

Tins and buns or tens and ones, it all works exactly the same way! Just pretend that the ten frames are muffin tins, and you'll do great!

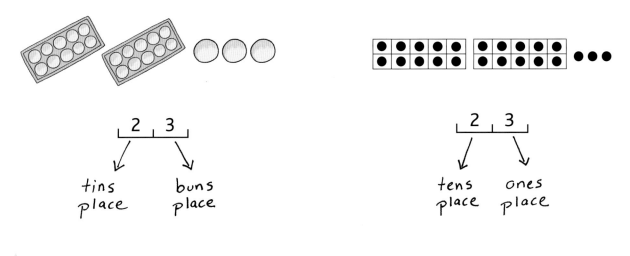

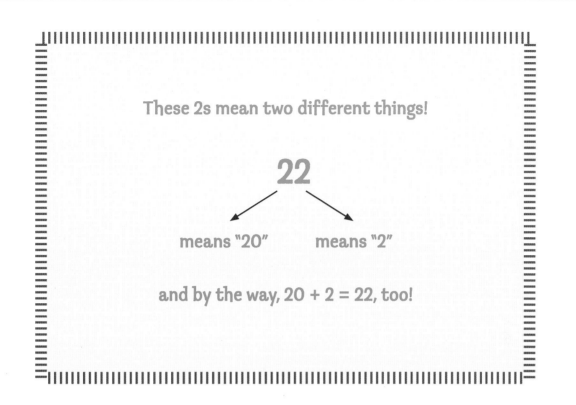

These 2s mean two different things!

22

means "20"   means "2"

and by the way, 20 + 2 = 22, too!

BOY, I GUESS YOU JUST CAN'T TRUST NUMBERS!

EXCUSE ME?

YOU CAN NEVER TELL WHAT A NUMBER IS WORTH! I MEAN, WHAT DOES IT STAND FOR? IS A 2 JUST A 2, OR IS IT 20? OR 200?

WE JUST LEARNED THAT WE *CAN* TELL-- BASED ON ITS PLACE VALUE!

WHATEVER YOU SAY. BUT I'M SLEEPING WITH ONE EYE OPEN TONIGHT.

Now, instead of tins and buns, let's play the same game with tens and ones.

How many tens? How many ones? Can you write the total?

I'll do the first one for you!

1. 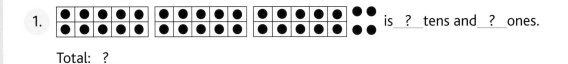 is __?__ tens and __?__ ones.

   Total: __?__

Let's Play: Hmm, we see three big tens—kind of like muffin tins!—so there must be **3** tens, and we see four leftover dots, so that's **4** ones, and that means we have **34** dots total!
Answer: **3** tens and **4** ones. Total: **34**

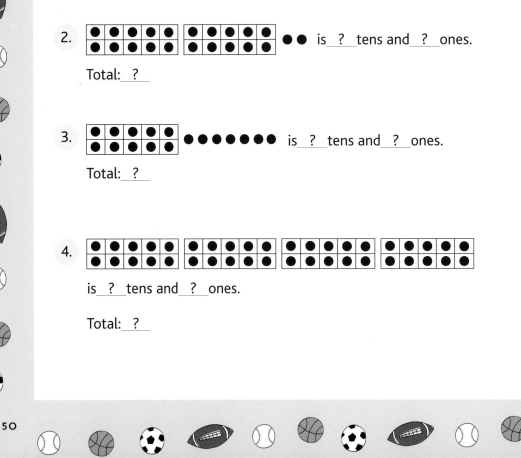

2. is __?__ tens and __?__ ones.

   Total: __?__

3. is __?__ tens and __?__ ones.

   Total: __?__

4. is __?__ tens and __?__ ones.

   Total: __?__

Can we figure out how many tens and how many ones there are just by looking at a number? Yes, we can! This is just like the game we played on page 47, but using tens and ones instead of tins and buns! I'll do the first one for you.

1.   60 is __?__ tens and __?__ ones.

Let's Play: Well, I see a 6 in the tins place—I mean, tens place—so there must be 6 tens, and since there's a 0 in the ones place, there must not be any leftover ones!
Answer: 60 is 6 tens and 0 ones.

2.   36 is __?__ tens and __?__ ones.   3.   63 is __?__ tens and __?__ ones.

4.   59 is __?__ tens and __?__ ones.   5.   12 is __?__ tens and __?__ ones.

6.   45 green birds. How many birds does the 5 stand for?

7.   82 purple hippopotamuses. How many hippopotamuses does the 8 stand for?

8.   58 orange monkeys. How many monkeys does the 8 stand for?

9.   50 brown cubs. How many cubs does the 5 stand for?

(Answers on pages 146–147.)

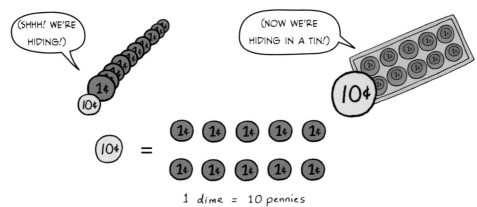

Cha-Ching: Pennies and Dimes!

Shiny coins are so pretty—and some are pretty sneaky! Pennies are worth 1 cent each, and **1 dime = 10 cents**. Each dime has the power of 10 pennies behind it . . . and what if those pennies were all hiding back there, in a tin?

1 dime = 10 pennies

If we had 10 buns, we'd put them in a tin, right? Well, if we had 10 pennies, we could trade them in for a dime! And that means 20 pennies is the same as 2 dimes, 30 pennies is the same as 3 dimes, and so on! Dimes are so great because they are even smaller than pennies, but they are worth so much more!

Let's pretend we have a huge pot in front of us, filled with dimes and pennies, and somebody told us to get 32 cents. I mean, sure, we could grab 32 pennies, but it would take forever to count all those pennies, and dimes are so much nicer, don't you agree? How many dimes should we grab, and how many pennies? Well, because 1 dime = 10 pennies, we can write 32 like this:

$$\underset{\substack{\text{number} \\ \text{of dimes}}}{3} \, \underset{\substack{\text{number} \\ \text{of pennies}}}{2}$$

Nice! So we could grab 3 dimes and 2 pennies. WAY easier than counting out 32 pennies.

This is a fun trick—but it only works because 10 pennies = 1 dime! (We'll learn more about money on page 65, in Chapter 4.)

TRY THIS: Get a big pile of pennies and dimes, and see how many ways you can make each of the numbers in the Game Time on page 54. For example, 21 cents could be 2 dimes and 1 penny, or 1 dime and 11 pennies, or just 21 pennies!

Pennies are pretty; pennies are great.

But using them takes too much time.

If I only used pennies, I'd always be late!

Oh, won't somebody give me a dime?

Counting by Tens with Dimes!

Since dimes are worth 10 cents each, whenever we see dimes, we can easily find out how much money we have by just counting by tens! So if we have 6 dimes, we'd count 10, 20, 30, 40, 50, **60 cents!**

GAME TIME!

Imagine a huge pot filled with dimes and pennies. How many of each coin should we take from the pot in order to use the *most* dimes possible? Draw on your paper, too, and count it out to make sure it works.

I'll do the first one for you!

1. 54 cents

Let's Play: Okay, let's write this ourselves: We see 4 in the ones (pennies) place, and 5 in the tens (dimes) place, so that means we need 5 dimes and 4 pennies! Let's draw them out:

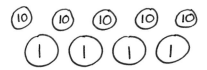

Now let's make sure we really have 54 cents. Counting by tens for the 5 dimes, we get "10, 20, 30, 40, 50." And then we count by ones to add the pennies, starting after 50: 51, 52, 53, 54. Yep, it worked—we have 54 cents!
Answer: 5 dimes and 4 pennies

2. 21 cents

3. 34 cents

4. 45 cents

5. 67 cents

6. 50 cents

7. 18 cents

(Answers on page 147.)

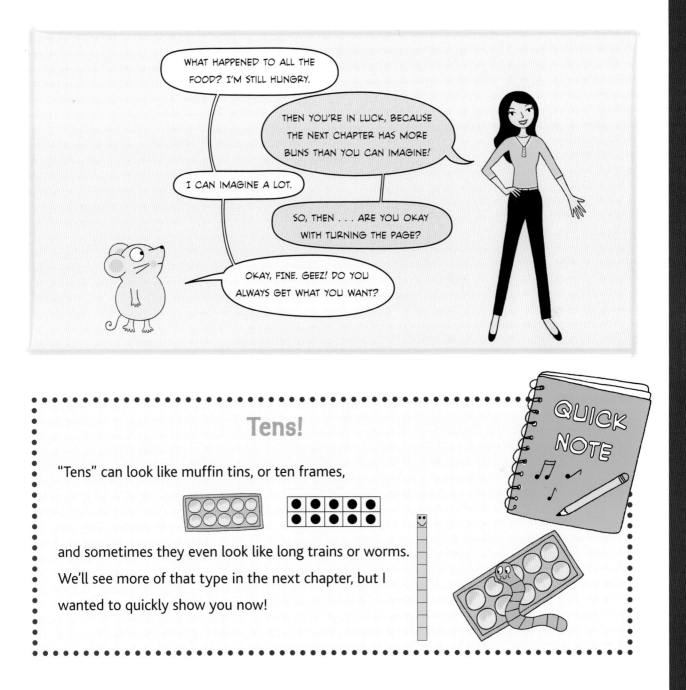

Tens!

"Tens" can look like muffin tins, or ten frames,

and sometimes they even look like long trains or worms. We'll see more of that type in the next chapter, but I wanted to quickly show you now!

Chapter 4

Buns, Not Butts!

The Hundreds Place and Three-Digit Numbers

Business Is Booming:
Place Value with Hundreds—Tonbreads!

As Lin and Larry's bakery got more and more popular, and their orders grew bigger and bigger, they started using long, skinny tins to hold 10 buns each, which looked like this:

Why did they change the type of tins? Because it was easier to bundle them together for big orders! In fact, they started having to bundle 10 of the tins together—which made the shape of a huge, flat square:

> NOW THAT'S A TON OF BREAD RIGHT THERE!

> TONBREAD . . .

Since buns are a type of bread, Lin and Larry decided to call each of these huge square packages a "ton of bread." But they didn't want to have to say three separate words, so they shortened it to "tonbread."

> THEY CAN'T EVEN SAY THREE WORDS? WOW, THAT'S PRETTY LAZY. . . . WAIT! "TONBREAD"? THAT SOUNDS A LOT LIKE "HUNDRED"!

> YES, MR. MOUSE, YOU ARE VERY SMART. AND THAT'S EXACTLY WHY WE'RE CALLING THESE BIG SQUARES "TONBREADS": IT TAKES ONE *HUNDRED* BUNS TO FILL A "TONBREAD" SQUARE! YEP, 100 BUNS!

> WOW . . . THAT'S A LOT OF BUTTS-- I MEAN, BUNS. JUST KIDDING. SORT OF. NOT REALLY. (PAUSE.) BUTT.

Here we can see how 10 tins is *the same amount as* 1 tonbread. In other words, 10 tens is the same as 1 hundred!

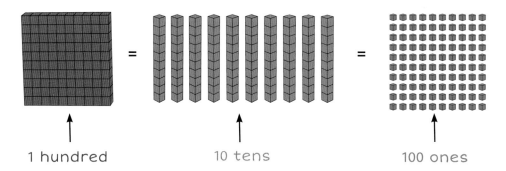

1 hundred   10 tens   100 ones

1 tonbread = 10 tins = 100 buns

HEY, I THINK THOSE ARE THREE WAYS OF SAYING THE SAME AMOUNT OF BUNS. THEY ALL HAVE 100 BUNS FOR PEOPLE TO EAT, RIGHT?

YEP! AND WE CAN DO THE SAME THING WITH JUST MATH WORDS: 100 ONES = 10 TENS = 1 HUNDRED.

THOSE THREE THINGS ARE SAYING THE SAME THING?

THEY'RE SAYING THE SAME AMOUNT--JUST GROUPED DIFFERENTLY.

2 tonbreads *is the same as* **200 buns**

3 tonbreads = 300 buns

4 tonbreads = 400 buns

. . . and so on. Can you see the pattern? How many buns are in 5 tonbreads? Yep—500 buns! Can you figure out the rest? Say them out loud!

6 tonbreads = _?_ buns   8 tonbreads = _?_ buns

7 tonbreads = _?_ buns   9 tonbreads = _?_ buns

Can we tell how many total buns there are below? Yep! It works the same way as tins and buns—we just have tonbreads now, too!

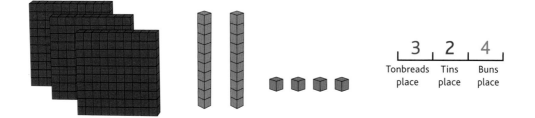

3	2	4
Tonbreads place	Tins place	Buns place

And we get a total of 324 buns. Easy, right? Let's play some games!

DON'T--

BUTT.

YOU BROUGHT THIS ON YOURSELF.

Buns vs. Ones

We've been using "tonbreads," "tins," and "buns" because they can make it easier to think about place value. But you probably won't see those words outside this book. So if you want, you can use "hundreds," "tens," and "ones" when you are writing out numbers in the following exercises—or you can stick with our buns for now. Totally up to you!

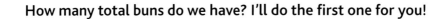

GAME TIME!

How many total buns do we have? I'll do the first one for you!

1.

Let's Play: Look at all those buns!! I'm so glad we don't have to count them all! How many tonbread squares do we have? 2! So a **2** goes in the tonbreads (hundreds) place. How many tins do we have? Counting them carefully, we get 8! So we put **8** in the tins (tens) place. And it looks like we don't have any extra buns. In other words, we have 0 extra buns. That means we put a **0** in the buns (ones) place. So we get **280**, "two hundred eighty." Great job!

Answer: 280 total buns

$$\underline{2,8,0}$$
hundreds tens ones

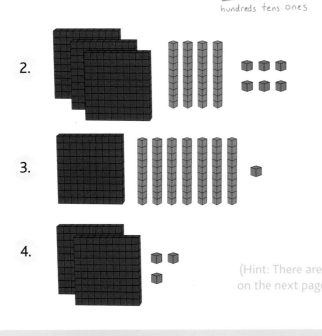

2.

3.

4.

(Hint: There are 0 tens! See Watch Out! on the next page for help if you need it!)

(Answers on page 147.)

For #4 on the previous page, what if we hadn't put a zero in the tens place? Let's say we'd written this, thinking, "Well, I see 2 hundreds and 3 ones and that's it!"

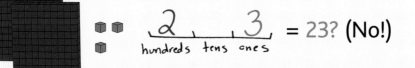

= 23? (No!)

Oops! If we don't write SOMETHING in the tens place, we might end up with the wrong answer, 23, which is way less than the real answer!

Instead, we need to do this: $\underline{2 \quad 0 \quad 3}$ = 203 (Yes!)
hundreds tens ones

The actual answer is 203. Yep, 203 buns!

Just to compare, here's what 23 looks like in pictures:

JUST WHEN I WAS STARTING TO TRUST NUMBERS AGAIN!

WHAT DO YOU MEAN?

THIS CRAZY ZERO THING!

LOOK, FOR 203, WE HAD NO TENS, RIGHT? SO WE PUT THE "NOTHING" NUMBER--ZERO-- IN THE TENS PLACE. SIMPLE AS THAT. YOU'RE GONNA DO GREAT!

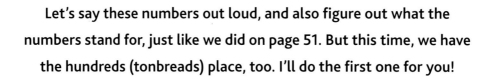

GAME TIME!

Let's say these numbers out loud, and also figure out what the numbers stand for, just like we did on page 51. But this time, we have the hundreds (tonbreads) place, too. I'll do the first one for you!

1. Say this out loud: "706 green frogs."
   How many frogs does the 7 stand for?

Let's Play: Okay, I know you can't hear me, but it would sound like "**seven hundred six frogs.**" Next part? Hmm, let's see—the 6 is in the ones (buns) place, so it stands for just 6 frogs, right? The 0 is in the tens (tins) place, so we put a zero there! And the 7 is in the hundreds (tonbreads) place, so it stands for **700** frogs, and that's our answer. Can you picture what this would look like?

$$\underline{706}$$
hundreds tens ones

That's a lot of frogs! (Don't tell Mr. Mouse.)
Answer: You would say "seven hundred six green frogs."
The 7 stands for 700 frogs.

2. 290 gray kittens. How many kittens does the 9 stand for?

3. 843 white mice. How many mice does the 8 stand for?

4. 158 pink ponies. How many ponies does the 8 stand for?

5. 672 yellow giraffes. How many giraffes does the 7 stand for?

Talking on the Phone: Digits!

Do you know your parents' phone numbers, just in case of an emergency? It's a good idea to memorize them! Most phone numbers are 10 **digits** long—3 digits for an area code, plus 7 digits for the rest of the number. What's a *digit*, you ask?

A **digit** is any numeral from 0 to 9. For example: What *digit* is in the tens place of 872, and how much does it stand for? Answer: **7** is in the tens place, and it stands for **70**. Easy, right?

I CAN'T WAIT TO GET MY OWN PHONE SOMEDAY. I WONDER WHAT THE DIGITS OF MY PHONE NUMBER WILL BE?

QUICK NOTE

The digit all the way to the right of a number is the ones place, then move left to the tens place, then left to the hundreds place, if it's a three-digit number. A single digit only has the ones place!

tens place ↘   ↙ ones place
16

tens place ↓
hundreds place → **509** ← ones place

8 ← ones place!

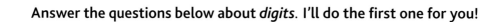

GAME TIME!

Answer the questions below about *digits*. I'll do the first one for you!

1. What digit is in the tens place of 804? How much does it stand for?

Let's Play: Starting from the right, we see that a 4 is in the ones place (and it just stands for 4), a 0 is in the tens place, and an 8 is in the hundreds place (and it stands for 800). So how much does the 0 in the tens place stand for? Well, no matter where a 0 is, it always stands for nothing!

Answer: 0, and it stands for 0.

2. What digit is in the ones place of 79? How much does it stand for?

3. What digit is in the hundreds place of 361? How much does it stand for?

4. What digit is in the tens place of 950? How much does it stand for?

5. What digit is in the hundreds place of 804? How much does it stand for?

6. What digit is in the tens place of 86? How much does it stand for?

7. What digit is in the ones place of 270? How much does it stand for?

8. What digit is in the ones place of 9? How much does it stand for?

9. What digit is in the hundreds place of 601? How much does it stand for?

(Answers on page 147.)

More Cha-Ching: Place Value with Dollars

Remember back on page 52 when we played around with pennies and dimes, and noticed that a dime is sort of like a tin (with 10 pennies in it)? Well, a dollar is like 100 pennies! Yes, a dollar is a lot like a tonbread. . . .

1 dollar = 10 dimes = 100 pennies

It's like each dollar is hiding a tonbread full of 100 pennies behind it! Can you imagine that? Yes, a dollar *is worth the same amount* of money as 100 pennies!

And it's pretty clear that dollars are a lot easier to count than all those pennies! So if we were at the store and somebody tried to give us 315 pennies for our change, we'd be like, "Hey, this is taking too long, and I don't want all those pennies! Instead, please give me 3 dollars, 1 dime, and 5 pennies, thank you very much."

And that makes it easier to see!

Remember, this only works for dollars, dimes, and pennies (not nickels or quarters!) because:

1 dollar = 10 dimes   and   **1 dime = 10 pennies**

just like   1 hundred = 10 tens   and   1 ten = 10 ones

If somebody handed you a big pile of pennies, what could you trade them in for, using dollars and dimes, to have the fewest possible number of things to count? *Hint: Start with dollars, use as many of those as you can, move to dimes, and finally pennies.* I'll do the first one for you!

Use this to help you figure out which digit goes in each place:

```
 |_____|_____|
dollars  dimes  pennies
 place   place   place
```

1. 406 pennies

Let's Play: First, we'll look at what we have in each place.

$$4 , 0 , 6$$
dollars dimes pennies

Notice that we have a 4 in the hundreds/dollars place (which equals 400 pennies!), so we could use 4 dollar bills instead for that. Next we have a 0 in the tens/dimes place, so we don't need any dimes. And finally, we have a 6 in the ones/pennies place, which means we need 6 pennies to finish it off. Answer: 4 dollars and 6 pennies

Remember to think of this as you do these!

```
 |_____|_____|
dollars  dimes  pennies
 place   place   place
```

2. 524 pennies

3. 867 pennies

4. 201 pennies

5. 980 pennies

(Answers on page 147.)

Dollars and Cents!

When we write about money, instead of writing . . .

$$4 \quad 0 \quad 6$$

dollars place   dimes place   pennies place

. . . we could write **$4.06** to express the same thing. Notice that we add a little dot called a decimal point between the dollars and the cents, and we write a "$," called a dollar sign, in front of the whole thing. When we see the "$," we say "dollars"—but we say it *after* the number. So for $4.06 we'd say "four dollars and six cents." And for $5.32, we'd say "five dollars and thirty-two cents." Just something good to know!

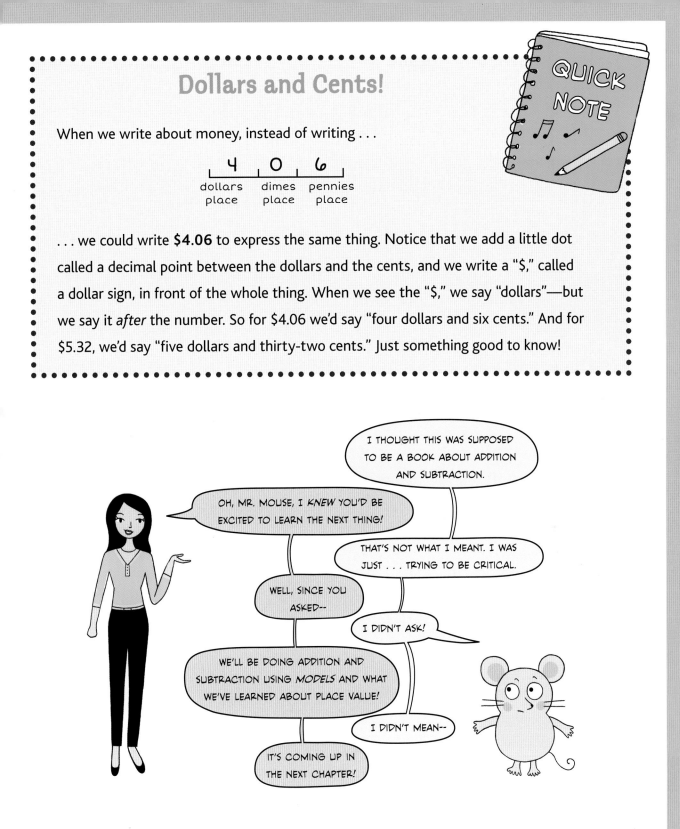

I THOUGHT THIS WAS SUPPOSED TO BE A BOOK ABOUT ADDITION AND SUBTRACTION.

OH, MR. MOUSE, I *KNEW* YOU'D BE EXCITED TO LEARN THE NEXT THING!

THAT'S NOT WHAT I MEANT. I WAS JUST . . . TRYING TO BE CRITICAL.

WELL, SINCE YOU ASKED--

I DIDN'T ASK!

WE'LL BE DOING ADDITION AND SUBTRACTION USING *MODELS* AND WHAT WE'VE LEARNED ABOUT PLACE VALUE!

I DIDN'T MEAN--

IT'S COMING UP IN THE NEXT CHAPTER!

Chapter 5

Strike a Pose!

Adding and Subtracting . . . with Models

Do you know what a **model** is? It's a person who puts on clothes and gets his or her picture taken to *show* everyone what the clothes *look like* on a person. When we are asked to "model" a number, that means to *show what it looks like* in pictures—in other words, draw a bunch of boxes like we saw in Chapter 4! So if we saw "Please model 243" in a math assignment, we could draw something like this (it's okay to draw ten sticks like French fries!):

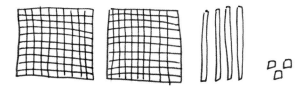

Just like before, the big squares stand for 100 each, the sticks stand for 10 each, and the baby squares stand for 1 each, so that's 243. (To draw a hundred, just make a big square, and then draw 9 little lines down and 9 little lines across!) They might not look as neat and tidy as the ones we saw in Chapter 4, but they work the same way. And now we're going to *add* with them!

Art Class: Using Models to Add Two-Digit Numbers

Let's say Lin has 23 buns, and Larry has 51 buns. How many total buns is that?

First, let's draw Lin's 23 buns! Just for fun, we'll color them in, too. We see a 2 in the tins place, so that's 2 tins, and a 3 in the buns place, so that's 3 extra buns:

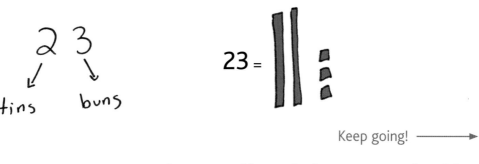

Keep going! ⟶

And how could we draw Larry's 51 buns? We see a 5 in the tins place, so that's 5 tins, and a 1 in the buns place, so that's 1 extra bun, right? We'll draw this:

We want to know how many <u>total buns</u> we have, so let's start by gathering the tins together. Lin had 2 blue tins, remember? And we can see Larry has 5 red tins. So that gives us 7 tins total, since 2 + 5 = 7, right?

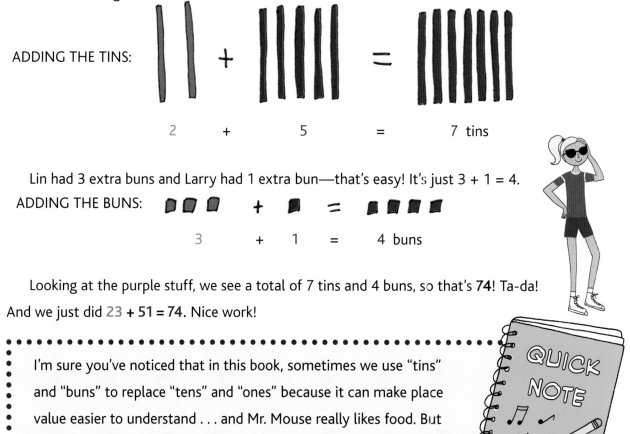

ADDING THE TINS:

2   +   5   =   7 tins

Lin had 3 extra buns and Larry had 1 extra bun—that's easy! It's just 3 + 1 = 4.
ADDING THE BUNS:

3   +   1   =   4 buns

Looking at the purple stuff, we see a total of 7 tins and 4 buns, so that's **74**! Ta-da! And we just did **23 + 51 = 74**. Nice work!

> I'm sure you've noticed that in this book, sometimes we use "tins" and "buns" to replace "tens" and "ones" because it can make place value easier to understand . . . and Mr. Mouse really likes food. But they both work! I'll do #1 on the next page using tens and ones, since that's what you'll see at school.

QUICK NOTE

GAME TIME!

Add together the two numbers by modeling the numbers—in other words, by drawing out the tins and buns. (Just rectangles and circles or baby squares are fine!) And then write out the full math sentence. I'll do the first one for you!

1.

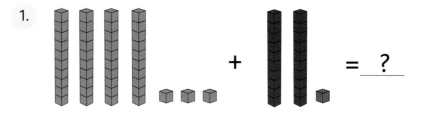

Let's Play: Okay, let's see what this is saying. In blue, we have 4 tens and 3 ones, so that's the number **43,** right? In red, we have 2 tens and I one, so that's **21.** We want to add 43 + 21, right? Great! First we'll ask: How many **total tens** do we have? 4 blue tens and 2 red tens make **6 tens** total, since 4 + 2 = 6. And then we ask: How many **total ones** do we have? 3 blue and I red make **4 ones** total, since 3 + 1 = 4! Let's put 'em together in a drawing:

That means we should put 6 in the tens place and 4 in the ones place, and we get **64!** The full math sentence would be 43 + 21 = 64.

Answer: 43 + 21 = 64 (and the picture we drew above)

Keep going! ⟶

2. + = ?

3. + = ?

4. + = ?

5. + = ?

(Answers on page 147.)

Hungry Mouse: Using Models to Subtract Two-Digit Numbers

Now we're going to look at subtraction with two-digit numbers, and we'll use tins and buns to help us! Let's say Lin has 8 tins and 6 extra buns—that's 86 buns total, right? And suddenly a very hungry mouse takes 3 tins and 4 of the extra buns when she wasn't looking. Wow! That means the mouse took *34* buns!

Here are the 86 buns we started with:

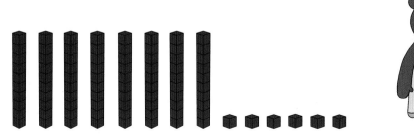

We cross out the 34 buns the mouse took and circle what's left over:

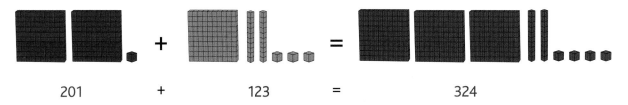

We're left with 5 tins and 2 extra buns, which is 52 buns total. And we've just done the subtraction problem: **86 − 34 = 52**. Not so bad, right?

Artist Extraordinaire: Using Models to Add and Subtract Three-Digit Numbers

Addition and subtraction with *three*-digit numbers works the exact same way!

For example, to figure out 201 + 123, we could do this:

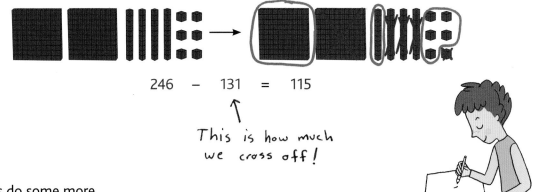

And to figure out 246 − 131, we could do this:

246 − 131 = 115

This is how much we cross off!

Ta-da! Let's do some more. . . .

GAME TIME!

First let's practice with two-digit numbers! How many buns did the mouse leave behind? To figure it out, draw the tins and buns (we'll "model" the numbers!), and cross off the parts the mouse ate. Then write the full math sentence. I'll do the first one for you!

1. We started with 54 buns, but the mouse ate 42 buns. How many are left?

Let's Play: This will be the subtraction problem **54 – 42**, right? To get the answer, first we'll write out **54** buns as 5 tins and 4 extra buns:

Next we'll take away **42** buns—in other words, we'll cross out 4 tins and 2 extra buns!

And we can see that we're left with 1 tin and 2 extra buns—in other words, we're left with 12 buns total! So the full math sentence is 54 – 42 = 12. Done!
Answer: 54 – 42 = 12

2. We started with 43 buns, but the mouse ate 11 buns. How many are left?

3. We started with 71 buns, but the mouse ate 20 buns. How many are left?

4. We started with 26 buns, but the mouse ate 13 buns. How many are left?

5. We started with 38 buns, but the mouse ate 17 buns. How many are left?

(Answers on page 147.)

Let's add and subtract three-digit numbers by drawing models and then writing out the full math sentence. I'll do the first one for you!

1. 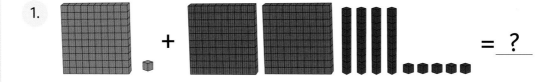 = ?

Let's Play: So, how many hundreds (tonbreads) do we see altogether? 1 blue and 2 reds = **3 hundreds** total. How many tens (tins) do we see? 0 blues and 4 reds = **4 tens** total. How many ones (buns) do we see? 1 blue and 5 reds = **6 ones** total. Let's draw it!

What is the full math sentence? First let's look back at the original problem:

Looking at just the blues, we see 1 hundred, 0 tens, and 1 one, so that's 101.

Looking at just the reds, we see 2 hundreds, 4 tens, and 5 ones, so that's 245.

And looking at our answer, we see 3 hundreds, 4 tens, and 6 ones, so that's 346.

So our math sentence is 101 + 245 = 346. Done!

Answer: 101 + 245 = 346 (and the neato picture we drew)

2. 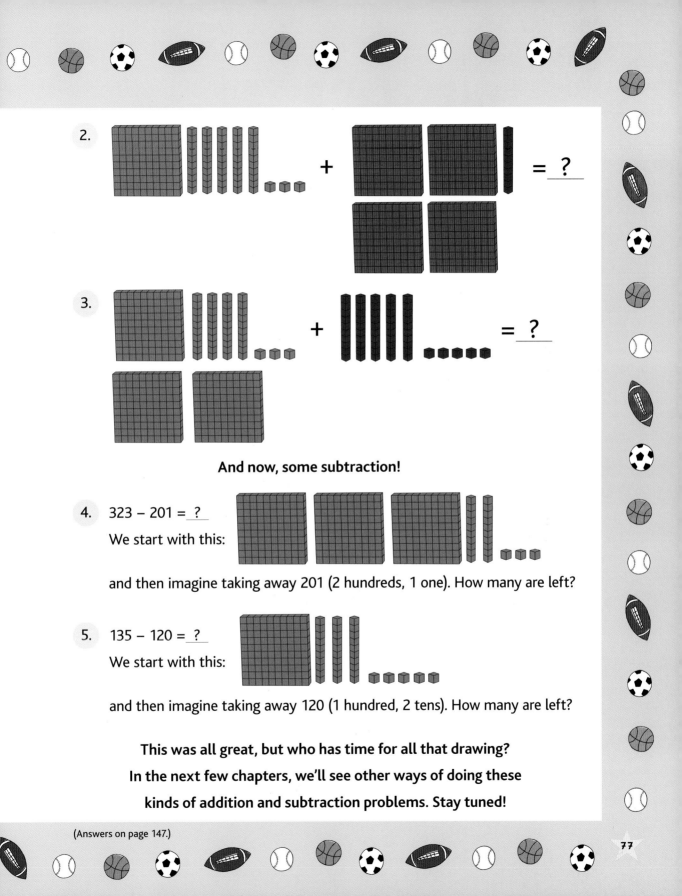 + = _?_

3. + = _?_

And now, some subtraction!

4. 323 − 201 = _?_
We start with this:

and then imagine taking away 201 (2 hundreds, 1 one). How many are left?

5. 135 − 120 = _?_
We start with this:

and then imagine taking away 120 (1 hundred, 2 tens). How many are left?

This was all great, but who has time for all that drawing?
In the next few chapters, we'll see other ways of doing these
kinds of addition and subtraction problems. Stay tuned!

(Answers on page 147.)

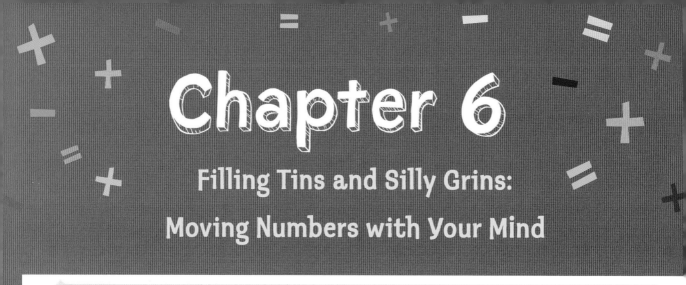

Chapter 6

Filling Tins and Silly Grins:
Moving Numbers with Your Mind

Just Like Magic:
Addition Up to 20, the Easy Way!

In this chapter, we're going to hang out with Lin and Larry again and fill their tins with buns—to start practicing addition and subtraction in our heads! So say we're going to work for Lin and Larry, putting buns into tins. We'd want to make sure we *filled up* the tins whenever we could, right?

For example, if someone wanted to buy 9 buns, and then wanted 5 *more* buns, we wouldn't want to hand over this:

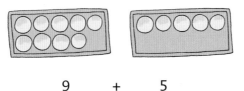

9   +   5

I mean, look at the tin on the left—doesn't it bug you that there's one space empty in it? It bugs me! We want *full tins* wherever possible. It looks much better, AND it makes it much easier to keep track of the total number of buns. So let's move one bun from the "5" to the "9."

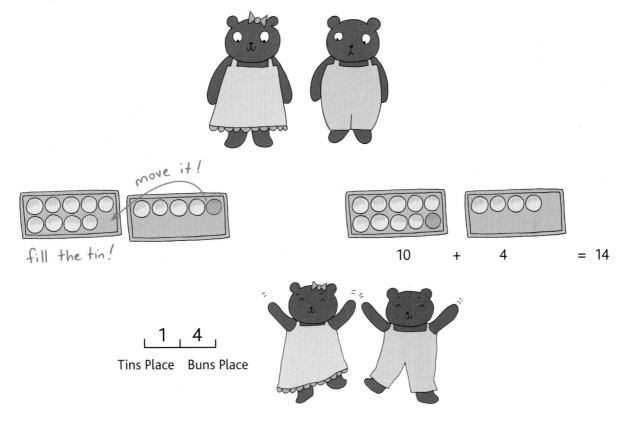

move it!

fill the tin!

10   +   4   = 14

1   4

Tins Place   Buns Place

Since all we did was move a bun, we didn't *change* the total number of buns we're selling, right? So that means 9 + 5 is the <u>same number of buns</u> as 10 + 4. Make sense? And we've "magically" turned **9 + 5** into the easy problem **10 + 4**, which is 14. Great!

It's usually easiest to fill up the tin that was already <u>closest to being full</u>. So in the problem on page 79, we moved **1 bun** from the "5" tin to fill up the "9" tin. Sure, we could have moved **5 buns** from the "9" tin to fill up the "5" tin, and we still would have ended up with 1 full tin and another tin with 4 buns, but moving fewer buns is easier.

Just so you know, the whole point of moving the buns to "fill a tin" is so we can turn these problems into the easy ones we saw in the chart on page 26, like **10 + 5 = 15** and **10 + 6 = 16.** By filling tins wherever we can, we'll be making the problems easy, like magic!

Said Larry to Lin, "It's easier, yup!

Filling the tins helps the numbers add up—

Each tin holds 10 buns like each ten has 10 ones!

This gets us the total—it's helping us tons!"

Filling a Tin and Making Ten

When we fill up a tin in order to turn it into an easier problem, we've put 10 buns in it, so most people call that "making ten" instead of "filling a tin." They mean the same thing! Our version is just a little tastier. . . .

Let's add two numbers together by "magically" turning them into easy problems first! How? By imagining we are moving buns to make one of the tins full! Then we'll write *both* math sentences shown. I'll do the first one for you!

(Just remember: first make 10—in other words, fill a tin!)

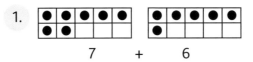

1.

$$7 \quad + \quad 6$$

Let's Play: Okay, we're supposed to "first make ten," which means we should move buns so that one of the tins is full. Let's imagine we take 3 buns out of the "6" tin and put them into the "7" tin. Here's the picture we'll imagine in our heads:

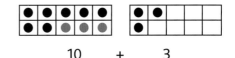

move!

fill the tin! $\quad 7 \quad + \quad 6 \qquad\qquad 10 \quad + \quad 3$

Now we have 10 (a full tin) and 3 leftover buns! Looks like 7 + 6 is the same thing as 10 + 3. We know 10 + 3 = 13 because that's so easy, and that must mean that 7 + 6 = 13, too!

Answer: 10 + 3 = 13, which means 7 + 6 = 13

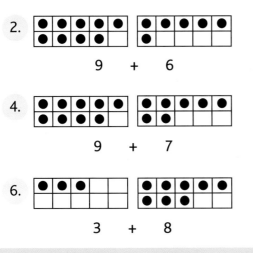

2.

$$9 \quad + \quad 6$$

4.

$$9 \quad + \quad 7$$

6.

$$3 \quad + \quad 8$$

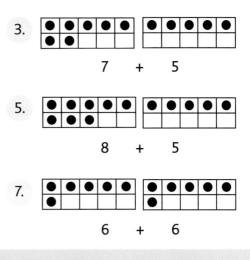

3.

$$7 \quad + \quad 5$$

5.

$$8 \quad + \quad 5$$

7.

$$6 \quad + \quad 6$$

(Answers on page 147.)

Not as Hungry Anymore: Subtraction Up to 20

Imagine someone wants to buy 15 buns, but then at the last second, she says, "Actually, can you take out 8 buns? I'm not that hungry after all."

How many will be left? This is the subtraction problem 15 − 8, right? Hmm, well, here are the **15** buns we start with:

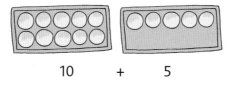

And now we're going to take away **8** buns, right? Okay. First, let's cross out the 5 buns that are in their own tin. I mean, who wants an extra empty tin lying around anyway? Okay, we've gotten rid of 5, so how many *more* do we need to cross out to take away a total of 8? We need to get rid of <u>3</u> more, since <u>3</u> + 5 = 8! See what I mean?

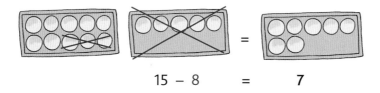

After crossing off 3 from the full tin, we're left with just **7** buns. We can also *imagine* crossing off buns from the tins, or even use our fingers to cover them up—whatever you like the most. This is a great way to think about these problems and to practice mental math!

GAME TIME!

Let's do these subtraction problems by imagining we are crossing off "buns."
We <u>always start by taking buns away from the emptier tin</u>, and then
see how many more buns we need to cross off from the full tin.
I'll do the first one for you!

1.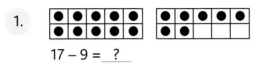

$17 - 9 = \underline{\ ?\ }$

Let's Play: In the picture, we can see what 17 buns looks like—we have 10 buns in the full tin, and 7 buns in the other tin. And now we have to get rid of 9 buns to figure out 17 – 9! Hmm, first we'll take away the 7 buns from the emptier tin—the one on the right. But to take off a *total* of 9, we still have to cross off 2 more buns from the full tin, right? Here's the picture we can imagine:

$$17 - 9 = $$

Or we can use our fingers to cover up those buns! And how many buns are left? We don't have to even count—since we took 2 buns away from 10, we know there must be *8* buns left over, since 10 – 2 = *8*.

Great! We've just done the problem: 17 – 9 = *8*. Done!
Answer: *8* buns

2.

$12 - 3 = \underline{\ ?\ }$

3.

$14 - 5 = \underline{\ ?\ }$

Keep going! ⟶

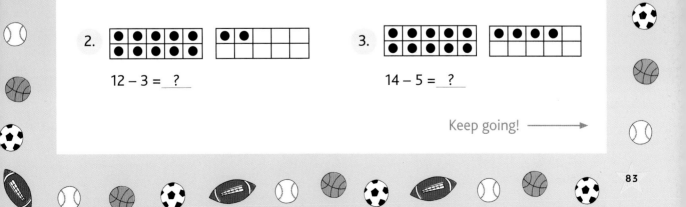

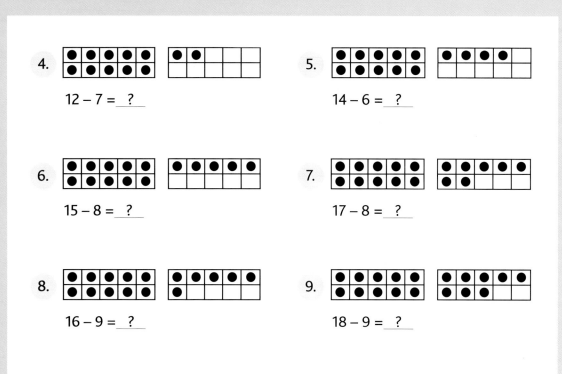

4. $12 - 7 = \underline{\ ?\ }$

5. $14 - 6 = \underline{\ ?\ }$

6. $15 - 8 = \underline{\ ?\ }$

7. $17 - 8 = \underline{\ ?\ }$

8. $16 - 9 = \underline{\ ?\ }$

9. $18 - 9 = \underline{\ ?\ }$

I LIKE SEEING MATH PROBLEMS INSIDE MY HEAD.

Practicing with ten frames (tins!) makes it easier for us to "see" addition and subtraction problems in our minds. Keep it up, and soon you'll be adding and subtracting like a champ!

(Answers on page 148.)

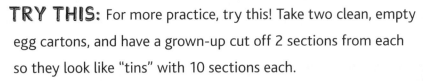

TRY THIS: For more practice, try this! Take two clean, empty egg cartons, and have a grown-up cut off 2 sections from each so they look like "tins" with 10 sections each.

Then use coins or other small objects to practice these kinds of problems. Or make up your own problems!

Upstairs and Downstairs: Adding and Subtracting 10 (and Groups of 10)

Whenever we add 10, all we're doing is adding a tin, right? For example, if we had 53 + 10, we could imagine that we start with 5 tins and 3 extra buns. To add 10, that's just adding 1 tin, which changes the 5 to a 6, and we get a total of 63!

We already know from Chapter 5 that we could *model* the problem like this:

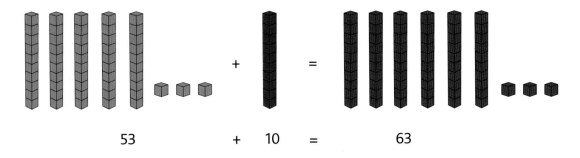

$$53 \quad + \quad 10 \quad = \quad 63$$

And notice that adding 1 ten means we just make the tens digit bigger by 1!

adding 10

$$\widehat{5}3 + 10 = \widehat{6}3$$

gets bigger by 1!

And subtracting 10 is just as easy!

Subtracting 10 is a lot like adding 10—but in order to *subtract* 10, we make the tens digit *smaller* by 1! Let's do 53 − 10, and look, we get 43!

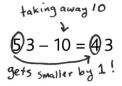

Hundred Chart

1	2	3	4	5	6	7	8	9	10
11	12	13	14	15	16	17	18	19	20
21	22	23	24	25	26	27	28	29	30
31	32	33	34	35	36	37	38	39	40
41	42	43	44	45	46	47	48	49	50
51	52	53	54	55	56	57	58	59	60
61	62	63	64	65	66	67	68	69	70
71	72	73	74	75	76	77	78	79	80
81	82	83	84	85	86	87	88	89	90
91	92	93	94	95	96	97	98	99	100

We can also look at this hundred chart—adding 10 means we go directly "downstairs" on the chart, and subtracting 10 means we go directly "upstairs." Like if we want to add 35 + 10, we look at the 35 and go downstairs to see that 35 + 10 = 45. Or to subtract 35 − 10, we'd go upstairs to see that 35 − 10 = 25.

Not so bad, right?

GAME TIME!

Let's add and subtract 10! You can either use the hundred chart on the previous page to move "downstairs" or "upstairs," or just think about making the digit in the tens place bigger or smaller by 1. I'll do the first one for you!

1. 93 – 10 = ___?___

Let's Play: Since we're subtracting 10, that's subtracting 1 from the tens digit, which is 9, right? Then the 9 becomes an *8* and the ones digit stays the same: so we get *83*! We also could have looked at the chart on page *86*—starting at 93 and going "upstairs" to subtract 10, we also end up at *83*!
Answer: 93 – 10 = 83

2. 68 + 10 = ___?___   3. 86 – 10 = ___?___

4. 45 + 10 = ___?___   5. 76 + 10 = ___?___

6. 87 – 10 = ___?___   7. 24 – 10 = ___?___

8. 16 + 10 = ___?___   9. 59 – 10 = ___?___

10. 91 – 10 = ___?___   11. 33 – 10 = ___?___

Yep, adding and subtracting 10 is pretty easy, because it's just a tin, after all! And guess what? Adding and subtracting *other numbers of tins* is pretty easy, too! So to subtract 54 – 20, we can imagine taking away *2 tins* from 5 tins so we're left with **3 tins**, right? And we still have **4** extra buns, so that's **34**! When you do these, just ask yourself, "How many tins do I have now? How many extra buns do I have?" And you'll do great!

(Answers on page 148.)

GAME TIME!

Let's add and subtract groups of 10—in other words, tins!

I'll do the first one for you.

1. 67 − 50 = _?_

Let's Play: With 67, we're starting with **6 tins** and 7 extra buns, and now we have to take **5 tins away.** That leaves us with just 1 tin! And the 7 extra buns stay just like they are: 67 − 50 = 17. Done!

Answer: 67 − 50 = 17

2. 45 + 20 = _?_

3. 98 − 30 = _?_

4. 34 + 10 = _?_

5. 78 − 40 = _?_

6. 29 + 70 = _?_

7. 41 + 50 = _?_

8. 56 + 40 = _?_

9. 66 − 60 = _?_

NICE JOB! AND GUESS WHAT? IN THE NEXT CHAPTER, WE'LL SEE EVEN MORE FUN TRICKS TO MAKE MATH EASIER!

(Answers on page 148.)

Chapter 7

Imaginary Friends:

Tricks to Make Addition Easier!

Have you ever had an imaginary friend? Or pretended that your room was a big castle or an airplane that you flew around the world? Those things take a lot of imagination! I'm going to show you some really great tricks we can use to make addition much easier, and our *imaginations* will be very helpful. . . . Let's do it!

Easy Addition Trick #1:
Using Our Imaginations to Make Ten!

In the last chapter, remember how we moved buns around in tins to "magically" turn problems into really easy ones, like on page 79, when 9 + 5 became 10 + 4? Now we'll do that without looking at tins and buns—we'll just use our imaginations! We can either imagine tins and buns, or we can imagine tens and ones. Let's try 7 + 5 = ?

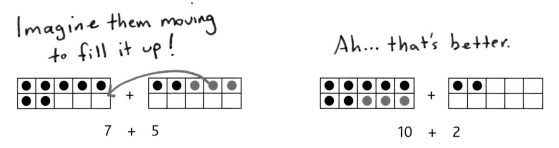

And just like that, we have discovered that 7 + 5 is the same as 10 + 2.

Now try 8 + 6, just in your mind. Imagine the two tens, and picture how many you'd need to move from the 6 to fill up the 8 ten. What are you left with once you fill it up? Can you fill in the blank?

8 + 6 is the same as 10 + ?

Give it a try on your own, and then check out #1 in our next Game Time and see how you did!

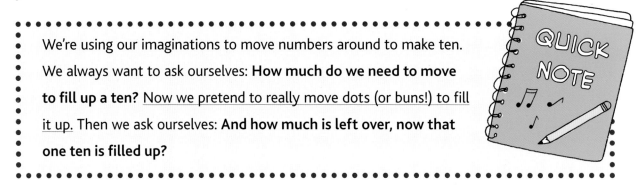

We're using our imaginations to move numbers around to make ten. We always want to ask ourselves: **How much do we need to move to fill up a ten?** <u>Now we pretend to really move dots (or buns!) to fill it up.</u> Then we ask ourselves: **And how much is left over, now that one ten is filled up?**

GAME TIME!

Use your imagination to fill up a tin, and turn this problem into an easy one!

(This is like what we did on page 81, but all in our heads this time!)

So we're not going to actually add them together; we're just *rewriting* them.

I'll do the first one for you!

1. 8 + 6 *is the same as* 10 + __?__

Let's Play: First imagine this as two tins—one with 8 buns and one with 6 buns. Can you see it? Good! Now, how many buns should we take from the "6" to fill up the "8" tin? Yep—2! Can you imagine them moving over to fill the tin? And that leaves us with 10 buns in one tin and 4 in the other tin. Great! And we've just shown that 8 + 6 is the same as 10 + 4. Ta-da! Let's write it out:

Answer: 8 + 6 is the same as 10 + 4

2. 9 + 5 *is the same as* 10 + __?__

3. 8 + 5 *is the same as* 10 + __?__

4. 9 + 7 *is the same as* 10 + __?__

5. 9 + 9 *is the same as* 10 + __?__

6. 3 + 8 *is the same as* 10 + __?__

7. 6 + 7 *is the same as* 10 + __?__

8. 8 + 7 *is the same as* 10 + __?__

9. 9 + 8 *is the same as* 10 + __?__

10. 6 + 5 *is the same as* 10 + __?__

11. 6 + 9 *is the same as* 10 + __?__

(Answers on page 148.)

Easy Addition Trick #2: Give and Take!

Have you ever given someone a present? Like, if you made them a card or picked out a toy for their birthday?

> I DON'T LIKE GIVING THINGS. I ONLY LIKE TAKING THINGS.

> THAT'S NOT VERY NICE!

> WELL, IT'S MORE FUN TO GET THINGS. I LIKE IT WHEN IT'S MY BIRTHDAY.

> I UNDERSTAND, BUT IT ALSO FEELS REALLY GOOD TO GIVE THINGS--LIKE WHEN YOU CAN'T WAIT FOR YOUR MOM OR DAD TO OPEN A PRESENT YOU GAVE THEM, BECAUSE YOU KNOW THEY WILL LOVE IT!

> I GUESS SO . . . BUT SOMETIMES IF I'M ON A PLAYDATE AND I'M NOT SHARING, MY MOM WILL TAKE A TOY FROM ME AND GIVE IT TO MY FRIEND.

> THAT'S PERFECT FOR WHAT WE'RE ABOUT TO LEARN!

Addition sure is easier when we use our imagination to "make 10," isn't it? Yay! Well, instead of imagining actual tins and buns, we can pretend that our two numbers are on a playdate and we need to help them share their toys better. I mean, if you have a friend over, the polite thing is to let them play with as many toys as they want, even if sometimes they have more toys in front of them than you do. In fact, let's be extra generous and always make sure they have 10 toys to play with. So, on a playdate, if one of the numbers is close to 10, we need to help them "Give and Take" their numbers to make it happen!

So if we want to add 8 + 7, we could pretend 8 and 7 are on a playdate. Let's *take* some of 7's toys to *give* to 8 so she can make 8 toy cars become 10. We could say to ourselves, "Hmm, 8 almost has 10! In order to *give* 2 to 8 (to get **10**), we need to *take* 2 from 7 (and get **5**)." So we've turned 8 + 7 into **10 + 5,** which is much nicer! Isn't it lovely when numbers play well together?

$$8 \quad + \quad 7$$
$$(give) \quad +2 \qquad -2 \ (take)$$
$$\downarrow \qquad \downarrow$$
$$10 \quad + \quad 5$$

We could either draw this picture, imagine this picture, or just *think* about the numbers changing. *Do what works best for YOU!*

GAME TIME!

Use your imagination to turn these into easier problems, and then do them!
You can imagine tins and buns or the "Give and Take" method—
whichever you want. Be sure to write out both math sentences at the end.
I'll do the first one for you!

1.   18 + 9 = __?__

Let's Play: Let's do the "Give and Take" method: we give
1 to the 9 (to make 10) and take 1 from the 18 (and it becomes
17).

$$18 + 9$$
$$\text{(take)} \quad -1 \quad +1 \quad \text{(give)}$$
$$\downarrow \qquad \downarrow$$
$$17 + 10$$

Writing both math sentences means we write 17 + 10 = 27 and
also 18 + 9 = 27. Done!
Answer: 17 + 10 = 27, which means 18 + 9 = 27

2. 9 + 5 = __?__

3. 9 + 6 = __?__

4. 8 + 7 = __?__

5. 17 + 8 = __?__

6. 8 + 18 = __?__

7. 7 + 4 = __?__

8. 6 + 16 = __?__

9. 9 + 9 = __?__

10. 7 + 6 __?__

11. 15 + 6 = __?__

(Answers on page 148.)

SHORTCUT ALERT!

EASY TRICKS FOR LEARNING
SOME OF THE FACTS

LOOK FOR DOUBLES!

Let's say we know our doubles facts from page 41, like 7 + 7 = 14, and we get a problem like 7 + 8. We might think, "Hey, this is 1 more than 7 + 7, so the answer must be 15!" Look out for addition problems that are near doubles facts *that you already know*. Your answer might be easier to get than you thought!

FINDING 10s

Sometimes we'll be asked to add three numbers together, like 3 + 6 + 7 = ? Sure, we could add 3 + 6 first (to get 9), and then add 9 + 7. Or we could look to see if any pairs of numbers add up to 10, and—yep!—since 3 + 7 = 10, and the order of addition doesn't change the answer, we can add 3 + 7 (to get 10) first.

$$10$$
$$3 + 6 + 7 = ? \quad \Rightarrow \quad 10 + 6 = ?$$

Then we can easily add 10 + 6 to get our answer, 16!

More Give and Take . . . with Bigger Numbers!

Let's do 53 + 38. Hmm, nobody is near 10, but 38 sure is near 40! In order to make 38 become **40,** we need to *give* 2 to it, which means we need to *take* 2 from 53, and it becomes **51.**

$$53 \quad + \quad 38$$
$$(\text{take}) \quad -2 \qquad +2 \ (\text{give})$$
$$\downarrow \qquad\qquad \downarrow$$
$$51 \quad + \quad 40$$

So we've turned 53 + 38 into **51 + 40**! And that's a much easier problem because we're just adding 4 tens to the 5 tens in 51, and that means we have a total of **9** tens with **1** extra one: 51 + 40 = **91.** Yep, we just showed that **53 + 38 = 91.** How about that!

By the way, with bigger numbers, it's ALWAYS a great idea to write out the "Give and Take" strategy. It's not like we're drawing pictures of muffin tins that would take forever; we're just showing our work, and that's a very good thing!

You might have noticed that there is more than one way to "Give and Take," depending on which number you want to end in 0. <u>But make sure that whatever amount you take from one number is the same amount you give to the other number!</u> For example, to add 41 + 28, we can't make them both end in 0, as tempting as it looks to try! Check it out:

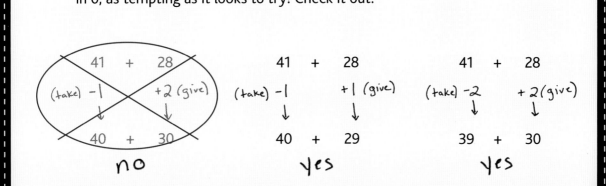

So both 40 + 29 and 39 + 30 give the right answer, which is 69! Remember, we're not changing the total number of toys here—that would change the answer! We're just moving the numbers around to make the addition look nicer and be easier to solve.

Isn't it nice, turning these addition problems into easier ones? So far, we've seen two ways of doing that. Trick #1 is to imagine our tins and buns, moving stuff around so we fill up a tin. Trick #2 is the "Give and Take" method we just saw. Now I'll show you Trick #3—where we do an easier problem first, and then fix the answer later! These are all great options for doing math in our heads—and it's up to you to decide which method you want to use. Let's do it!

Easy Addition Trick #3: Clean the Mess Later!

Have you ever been playing with your toys and then you want to go do something fun . . . but you really don't want to clean up the mess yet?

You might think, "Oh, *I'll do what I want now,* and then I'll just *clean up these messy toys later.*" Depending on how strict your parents are, that might or might not work very well for you! But we *can* do this with math—sort of.

Let's add 32 + 49. We could say to ourselves, "Gosh, 32 + 49 is messy. Instead, I'm going to do an easier version. I'm going to take away 2 from the 32 and do the easier problem 30 + 49, which is just 79. But that's not our final answer. We made a mess when we *took away 2*, and now we have to clean it up by *adding 2 back in* to get our real answer: 79 + 2 = **81**. Done!"

See how that works? There are so many ways to think about addition. <u>Use whichever ways you like most.</u> The point is to move around the numbers and turn the problem into an easier one—usually a problem that uses a number ending in 0.

GAME TIME!

Use your favorite method to add these numbers by first turning them into "easy" problems so one of the numbers ends in 0, like 10 or 20. I'll do the first one for you!

1. 65 + 17 = __?__

Let's Play: First we'll use the "Give and Take" method. The 17 is sort of close to 20—we just need to add 3, right? Time to share toys! Well, if we give 3 to the 17 to get 20, then we have to take 3 from the 65 to make 62.

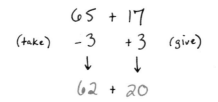

And that's much easier: 62 + 20 = 82! To "Clean the Mess Later," we could think, "Hmm, I don't want to do 65 + 17. I'd rather do 65 + 20! And that's 85." But since we added an extra 3, now we have to subtract 3 to get our final answer, and we get 82. Done!

Answer: 65 + 17 = 82

2. 65 + 11 = __?__

3. 22 + 38 = __?__

4. 33 + 9 = __?__

5. 19 + 13 = __?__

6. 16 + 68 = __?__

7. 84 + 7 = __?__

8. 59 + 13 = __?__

9. 28 + 13 = __?__

10. 12 + 47 = __?__

(Answers on page 148.)

A Word About Subtraction

The methods in this chapter only work for addition, *not subtraction*! In subtraction, we're finding the *difference* between two numbers, which is very different from combining two amounts. So when you see subtraction problems, only think about crossing out tins and buns—no playdates! ;)

As you know, the more you run, the better you get at it! Exercising your body makes your body stronger. Exercising your brain—by doing math—makes your brain stronger! Yep, you're making your brain stronger RiGHT NOW. (Good job!)

Chapter 8

Stretch, Kitty, Stretch!

Using Expanded Form for Addition and Subtraction

Have you ever watched a cat stretch? One minute she's a cute *little* kitty, and then suddenly she's *loooong.* It's the same cat, just stretched out! Well, we can do the same thing with numbers when we write them in **expanded form.**

I DON'T LIKE CATS.

THAT'S . . . BESIDES THE POINT.

I'M A MOUSE. I DON'T LIKE CATS. I DON'T LIKE--

MR. MOUSE!

I'LL STOP.

Stretch Out or Stand Up?
Expanded vs. Standard Form!

Remember when we talked about **digits** on page 63? When we write a number in *expanded form*, we just take each digit and show how much it stands for! It's like we're discovering what's *inside* a number and showing everyone how much it's really worth.

Expanded form:

87 = **80 + 7**

456 = **400 + 50 + 6**

222 = **200 + 20 + 2**

"Nothing" to Write!

When one of the digits is a zero, then *we don't need to write anything* for that place's value—the 0 stands for nothing! So for 906, instead of writing 906 = 900 + 0 + 6, we can just write **906 = 900 + 6**. Make sense?

QUICK NOTE

Writing numbers in expanded form can also help us remember how to say them out loud! After all, we say 456 out loud as "four hundred fifty-six," right? Check it out:

"four hundred   fifty-six"

400   +   50 + 6

GAME TIME!

You're a kitty and you want to stretch out! Write the following numbers (kitties) in expanded (stretched-out) form. I'll do the first one for you!

1. 809

Let's Play: We see an 8 in the hundreds place, so we know it's worth 800. We see a 0 in the tens place, but a 0 is worth 0, no matter where it is! We also see a 9 in the ones place, so we know that's just worth 9.

Should we write 800 + 0 + 9? Well, I guess we could, but we don't need the extra 0. Here we go . . . STRETCH . . . !
Answer: 809 = 800 + 9

2. 186

3. 324

4. 59

5. 425

6. 99

7. 311

8. 888

9. 567

10. 717

11. 950

12. 12

13. 501

(Answers on page 148.)

Standard Form and Expanded Form

??? WHAT'S IT CALLED? ???

To write a number in **expanded form** means to split it up to show how much *each digit stands for*. If a number is written normally (not in expanded form), then we say it's written in **standard form**. So 294 is in standard form, and 200 + 90 + 4 is the same number written in expanded form.

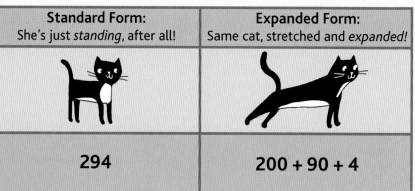

Standard Form: She's just *standing*, after all!	Expanded Form: Same cat, stretched and *expanded!*
294	200 + 90 + 4

I DON'T LIKE CATS, BUT I DO LIKE THAT WE'RE NOT DOING ANY "REAL" MATH LIKE ADDITION OR ANYTHING.

WELL, I'M GLAD YOU'RE FEELING HAPPY.

LET'S NOT GET CRAZY.

Now we're going to see the stretched-out kitties and figure out what they look like when they are just *stand*ing there . . . you know, in *standard* form.

GAME TIME!

Write each expanded number (stretched-out kitty) in standard form (as a standing kitty). I'll do the first one for you!

1. 600 + 70

Let's Play: Hmm, 600 means we want 6 in the hundreds place, and the 70 means we want 7 in the tens place, but what do we put in the ones place? We have to write *something* or we'll end up with 67, which is way smaller than the real answer. So what goes in the ones place? You guessed it: 0!

Answer: 670

2. 500 + 90 + 8   3. 700 + 40 + 6   4. 100 + 10 + 1

5. 600 + 10 + 9   6. 100 + 20 + 3   7. 900 + 80 + 7

8. 90 + 9   9. 900 + 30   10. 800 + 8

GUESS WHAT? YOU JUST DID ADDITION WITH THREE-DIGIT NUMBERS!

WAIT, YOU TRICKED ME?

SORT OF. AND YOU KNOW WHAT? I FEEL OKAY ABOUT THAT.

(Answers on page 148.)

Pile 'Em Up and Stretch 'Em Out: Adding and Subtracting Two-Digit Numbers in Expanded Form

We've talked about a few ways to do problems like 23 + 51. But now let's see how the kitties do it! Have you ever seen kittens snuggling, stretched out and lying on top of each other? It's so cute.

THAT'S TERRIFYING.

Well, numbers pile up and stretch out, too!

Let's make a kitty pile with 23 + 51 and stack them:

$$23$$
$$+\ 51$$

Now we'll stretch 'em out and add 'em up!

$$23 = 20 + 3$$
$$+\ 51 = 50 + 1$$
$$\overline{}$$
$$70 + 4 = 74$$

See? We can circle the numbers in the ones place together and add those up (3 + 1 = **4**), and then do the same thing for the tens place (20 + 50 = **70**). Then we just add **70 + 4 = 74**. And now we've shown that **23 + 51 = 74**. Nice job!

Look! It's kitties snuggled up and asleep on top of each other.

Let's stretch 'em out and add 'em up! I'll do the first one for you.

$$1. \quad 62$$
$$+ \ 21$$

Let's Play: First thing we'll do is rewrite the problem, and then stretch the kitties—I mean, numbers! So next to the 62, we'll write **= 60 + 2** and next to the 21, we'll write **= 20 + 1.**

$$62 = 60 + 2$$
$$+ \ 21 = 20 + 1$$

Then we'll add the ones together, and then the tens together. So 2 + 1 = **3**, and 60 + 20 = **80**. Then we'll unstretch them and put the answer back together in standard form. 80 + 3 = **83**. Done!

$$62 = \fbox{60} + \fbox{2}$$
$$+ \ 21 = \fbox{20} + \fbox{1}$$
$$80 + 3 = 83$$

Answer: **83**

2.	45	3.	34	4.	70
	+ 43		+ 25		+ 19

5.	61	6.	27	7.	58
	+ 16		+ 52		+ 30

Guess what? Subtraction works the same way!

Keep going! ⟶

Look, it's kitties again, snuggled up and asleep on top of each other. Subtract these by stretching 'em out and subtracting 'em! I'll do the first one for you.

1.   86
   − 30

Let's Play: Time for these kitties to stretch! And even though it seems strange, writing 30 as "30 + 0" helps remind us that 30 has 3 tins and 0 extra buns—and keeps everything straight!

$$86 = 80 + 6$$
$$- \ 30 = 30 + 0 \quad \downarrow \text{Subtract}$$

Next let's circle the ones place, subtract 6 − 0 = 6, then circle the tens place, and subtract 80 − 30 = **50**.

$$86 = \boxed{80} + \boxed{6}$$
$$- \ 30 = \boxed{30} + \boxed{0} \quad \downarrow \text{Subtract}$$
$$50 + 6 = 56$$

And finally, we just unstretch and put the kitty back together again! 50 + 6 = 56. Done!
Answer: 56

2.   53   ↓ Subtract
    − 21

3.   64   ↓ Subtract
    − 11

4.   98   ↓ Subtract
    − 36

5.   87   ↓ Subtract
    − 50

6.   72   ↓ Subtract
    − 61

7.   49   ↓ Subtract
    − 32

(Answers on page 149.)

Soon we'll do addition and subtraction *without* using expanded form, but for now, it can help us see what's really going on.

I LOVE IT WHEN MATH IS CUTE.

HEY, MR. MOUSE, WHAT DO YOU CALL A *REALLY* BIG PILE OF KITTENS?

I HAVE A FEELING YOU'RE GOING TO TELL ME.

A MEOWNTAIN! YOU KNOW, LIKE MOUNTAIN, BUT "MEOW" BECAUSE THEY'RE--

YES, I GET IT. AND NOW I'M GOING TO HAVE NIGHTMARES ABOUT BIG PILES OF CATS. HAPPY?

Stretch, Kitty, Stretch! Using Expanded Form for Addition and Subtraction

Meowntains: Adding and Subtracting Three-Digit Numbers in Expanded Form!

We can add three-digit numbers with expanded form, too! How about 235 + 461? Let's pile these kitties up, stretch 'em out, and add 'em up!

$$235 \quad \longrightarrow \quad 235 = 200 + 30 + 5$$
$$+ 461 \qquad\qquad\quad + 461 = 400 + 60 + 1$$
$$600 + 90 + 6 = \mathbf{696}$$

We just stretch out the numbers, making sure to keep all the hundreds digits together, the tens digits together, and the ones digits together. Circle 'em, and add! Just look at those cute little kitty piles. . . .

TIME TO PUT YOUR THINKING CAT ON!

GAME TIME!

Add these three-digit numbers by rewriting them and stretching out the kitties on the kitty pile! I'll do the first one for you.

1. 732 + 107

Let's Play: This might seem scary at first, but not if we think about our cuddly meowntain. First, we'll write the numbers on top of each other:

$$732$$
$$+107$$

. . . and then we stretch the kitties! Since there are 0 tens in 107, it's a good idea to put a 0 in that spot so we can keep everything straight when we're adding.

$$732 = 700 + 30 + 2$$
$$+ 107 = 100 + 0 + 7$$

Next we circle the hundreds together, the tens together, and the ones together, and add 'em together!

$$732 = \boxed{700} + \boxed{30} + \boxed{2}$$
$$+ 107 = \boxed{100} + \boxed{0} + \boxed{7}$$
$$800 + 30 + 9 = 839$$

How about that? Meow!

Answer: 839

2. 354
   + 534

3. 718
   + 160

4. 303
   + 492

5. 123 + 231
   (Hint: Stack them up!)

6. 426 + 551

7. 807 + 151

Now let's practice *subtracting* big piles of kitties!

Keep going! ⟶

GAME TIME!

Subtract these three-digit numbers by stretching out the kitties on the kitty pile! I'll do the first one for you.

1. 725 – 205

Let's Play: First, let's rewrite this as a kitty pile: Next we'll stretch these kitties out. . . .

$$\begin{array}{r} 725 \\ -\ 205 \\ \hline \end{array}$$

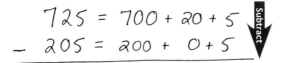

$$725 = 700 + 20 + 5$$
$$-\ 205 = 200 + 0 + 5 \quad \text{Subtract} \downarrow$$

Then we circle the hundreds together, the tens together, and the ones together, and subtract down!

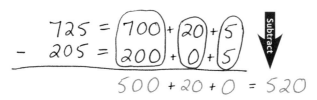

$$725 = \boxed{700} + \boxed{20} + \boxed{5}$$
$$-\ 205 = \boxed{200} + \boxed{0} + \boxed{5} \quad \text{Subtract} \downarrow$$
$$500 + 20 + 0 = 520$$

Finally, we take the expanded 500 + 20 + 0 and put it back together as **520**. Nicely done!

Answer: **520**

2.	847	3.	589	4.	564
	– 612		– 478		– 152

5. 980 – 430
(Hint: Stack them first like we did in #1!)

6. 673 – 142

7. 438 – 333

(Answers on page 149.)

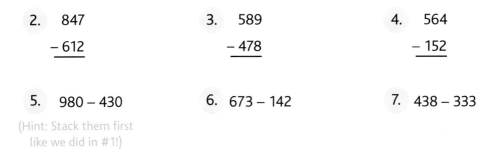

A Faster Way: Adding and Subtracting *Without* Expanded Form!

I'm going to let you in on a little secret—while our meowntains have been adorable and everything, there's a *faster* way to add and subtract. . . .

SHORTCUT ALERT!

THREE WAYS TO ADD + SUBTRACT

You know what's better than having to draw pictures for everything? Writing stuff in expanded form. You know what's better than writing stuff out in expanded form? Just writing the answer! Here's a comparison of the three different ways we can do this problem:

$$361 + 124 = 485$$

With pictures:

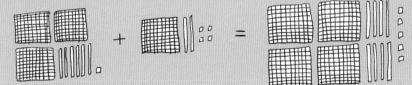

Wow, that's a lot of drawing! Here's that same problem, but using our stretching-kitty expanded form instead of drawing pictures:

Stretch, kitties!

$$\begin{array}{r} 361 = 300 + 60 + 1 \\ + \quad 124 = 100 + 20 + 4 \\ \hline 400 + 80 + 5 = 485 \end{array}$$

And here's that same problem *again*, the shortest way (shortcut!):

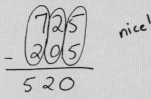

wow, that's quick!

$$\begin{array}{r} 3\,6\,1 \\ +\ 1\,2\,4 \\ \hline 4\ 8\ 5 \end{array}$$

All we do is <u>add directly down</u> in each column, and we always start with the ones place. So we'll do: 1 + 4 = **5** in the ones place, 6 + 2 = **8** in the tens place, and 3 + 1 = **4** in the hundreds place. We can circle them, but we don't have to!

And here's how the shortcut looks for the subtraction problem we did in #1 on page 112:

nice!

$$\begin{array}{r} 7\,2\,5 \\ -\ 2\,0\,5 \\ \hline 5\ 2\ 0 \end{array}$$

We just subtract down in each column: 5 − 5 = **0** in the ones place, 2 − 0 = **2** in the tens place, and 7 − 2 = **5** in the hundreds place. So much faster, right?

This last method is the fastest, but everybody is different, so see which method you like the most and use that one.

Can you feel your brain getting stronger?

IF THERE'S SUCH A GREAT SHORTCUT, THEN WHY ON EARTH DID YOU HAVE US DOING ALL THAT DRAWING? AND *WHY* BRING CATS INTO IT?

THE REASON WE DO ALL THE OTHER STUFF IS BECAUSE WHEN WE'RE ADDING OR SUBTRACTING BIG NUMBERS, IT'S HELPFUL TO KNOW WHAT'S REALLY HAPPENING IN TERMS OF PLACE VALUE. LIKE ON PAGE 114, WHEN WE SUBTRACTED 7 − 2 IN THE HUNDREDS COLUMN, WE WERE REALLY SUBTRACTING 700 − 200. KEEP THAT IN MIND, AND YOU'LL DO GREAT!

When we see a problem like 732 + 61 with different numbers of digits, it can be tricky to line everything up correctly, and if we don't, we might get the wrong answer!

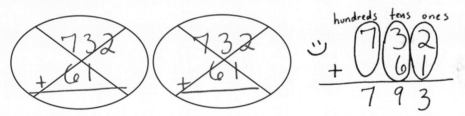

So we should always ask, "Which digits are in the ones place?" Here, it's the 2 and 1, so we'd make sure they are stacked up, kitty-style. "Which digits are in the tens place?" Here, it's the 3 and 6, so we should make sure they're lined up, too. Then we can add directly down in each column and we get the right answer! See what I mean? Also, notice that since we had 7 hundreds to start off with, and we didn't add any hundreds, we still have 7 hundreds in the answer.

GAME TIME!

Add and subtract without pictures and without expanding anything out.

I'll do the first one for you!

1. 875 − 72 = ?

Let's Play: We'll start by stacking them up and making sure they're all lined up. Which digits are in the ones place? 5 and 2. Which digits are in the tens place? Both 7s. So we'll make sure those pairs are stacked!

We always start with the ones place, so 5 − 2 gives us **3**. Then 7 − 7 gives us **0** in the tens place. And finally, since we're not subtracting anything in the hundreds place, we'll end up with **8** hundreds in the answer, and so we just write the **8** below! Done!

Answer: **803**

2. 652
    + 134

3. 874
    − 532

4. 768
    − 414

5. 707
    − 404

6. 890 − 390

7. 508 − 507

8. 542 + 346

9. 987 − 654

10. 324 + 72

11. 987 − 231

12. 26 + 43

13. 865 − 805

(Answers on page 149.)

Chapter 9

Freeway Driving and Piggyback Rides:
Addition with Regrouping (aka "Carrying")

Have you noticed that when your parents are driving, the cars and trucks mostly stay in their own lanes? That helps to keep them from crashing into each other, which is a very good thing.

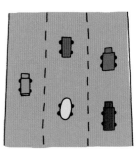

We're going to use the same method to keep our place values straight for adding big numbers!

On page 115, we did 732 + 61, circling the ones together and the tens together. That made it easier to keep the numbers in the right spots. But we could also make it look more like a freeway, and draw in lanes!

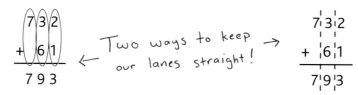

Two ways to keep our lanes straight!

$$
\begin{array}{r}
7\ 3\ 2 \\
+\ \ 6\ 1 \\
\hline
7\ 9\ 3
\end{array}
$$

Isn't it nice to have choices? As the problems get more challenging, I prefer the freeway lanes, especially as the numbers start riding around on each other's shoulders and playing piggyback.

HUH?

YOU HEARD ME-- PIGGYBACK!

Carry Meeeeeee!
Adding Two-Digit Numbers with Regrouping

When you were little, did you ever play piggyback, maybe on your parents' shoulders or an older sibling's back? You know, you climb up and they carry you? Pretty soon our numbers are going to do the same thing. . . .

What if we have something like this: 25 + 48? First we'll pile 'em up like snuggling kittens, and then write in the freeway lanes so everybody minds their own business and doesn't crash into each other.

$$
\begin{array}{r}
2\,|\,5 \\
+\ 4\,|\,8 \\
\hline
\end{array}
$$

At first it might seem like nothing special, but check it out: When we add the ones column, we get 5 + 8 = 13. Hmm, we can't write the entire 13 in the ones column or we'll get the wrong answer! Well, what is 13? It's 1 ten and 3 ones, right? So we put 3 in the ones column, and then we take the 1 ten, and we have it ride piggyback on top of the tens column! Because think about it: we've created a whole new ten, and it needs to go in the tens column—that's where it belongs.

$$
\begin{array}{r}
1 \\
2\,|\,5 \\
+\ 4\,|\,8 \\
\hline
|\,3
\end{array}
\qquad
\begin{array}{r}
1 \\
2\,|\,5 \\
+\ 4\,|\,8 \\
\hline
7\,|\,3
\end{array}
$$

And then we just add up the tens column: 1 + 2 + 4 = 7. For our answer, we get 7 tens and 3 ones, and that's **73**. Done!

We're going to call this *regrouping*, which is probably what they call it at your school. Some people—including your parents, maybe—call this "carrying."

Two-Digit Addition:
When Do We Regroup?

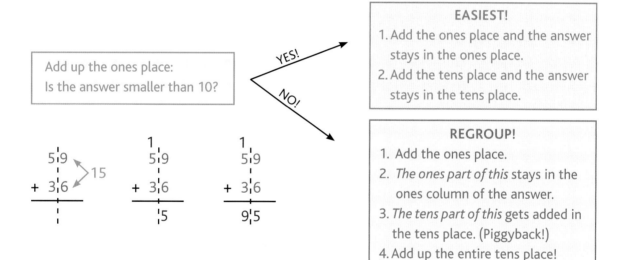

Add up the ones place:
Is the answer smaller than 10?

YES!

NO!

EASIEST!
1. Add the ones place and the answer stays in the ones place.
2. Add the tens place and the answer stays in the tens place.

REGROUP!
1. Add the ones place.
2. *The ones part of this* stays in the ones column of the answer.
3. *The tens part of this* gets added in the tens place. (Piggyback!)
4. Add up the entire tens place!

The Return of the Models . . . for Regrouping

Remember our models from Chapter 5? Let's do some drawing for regrouping!

How would we add 36 + 18 with models? First, we'd draw both numbers as models, right? We'll do that, but this time, we'll stack them like kitties, too. I'll show you the freeway version at the same time, just to compare them! Which way do you like more?

# Two Ways to Do 36 + 18

With Models

Freeway Lanes Only

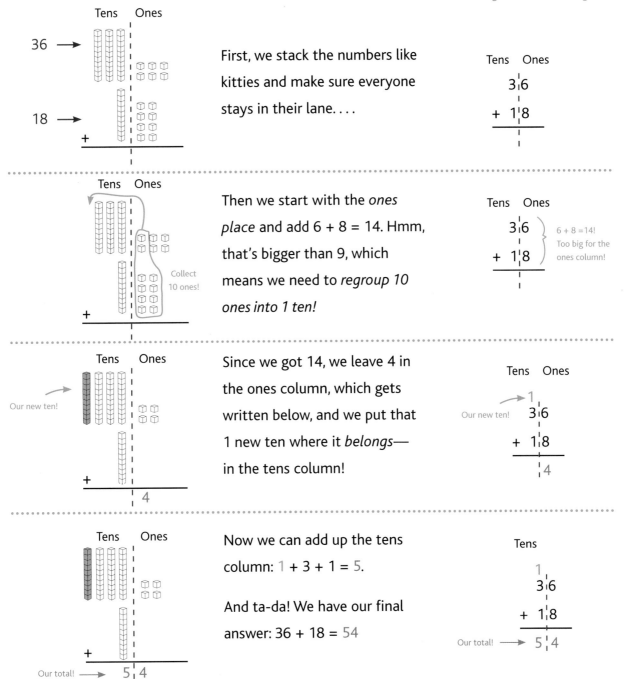

First, we stack the numbers like kitties and make sure everyone stays in their lane. . . .

Then we start with the *ones place* and add 6 + 8 = 14. Hmm, that's bigger than 9, which means we need to *regroup 10 ones into 1 ten!*

Since we got 14, we leave 4 in the ones column, which gets written below, and we put that 1 new ten where it *belongs*— in the tens column!

Now we can add up the tens column: 1 + 3 + 1 = 5.

And ta-da! We have our final answer: 36 + 18 = 54

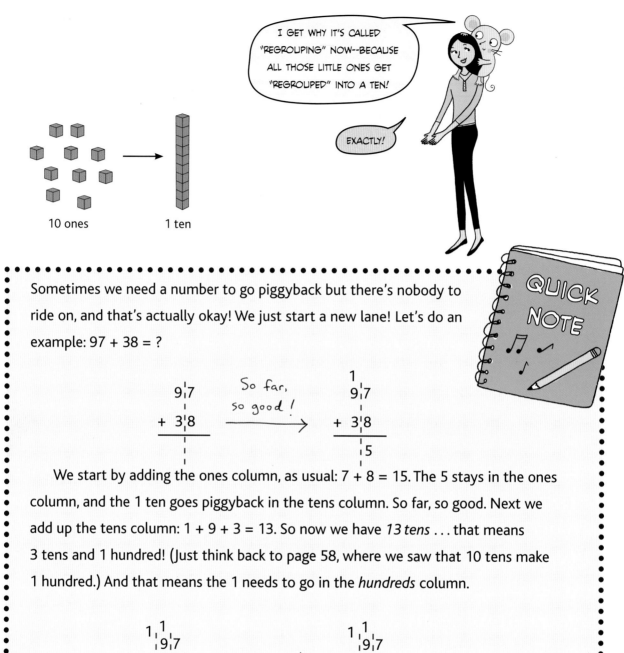

I GET WHY IT'S CALLED "REGROUPING" NOW--BECAUSE ALL THOSE LITTLE ONES GET "REGROUPED" INTO A TEN!

EXACTLY!

10 ones → 1 ten

QUICK NOTE

Sometimes we need a number to go piggyback but there's nobody to ride on, and that's actually okay! We just start a new lane! Let's do an example: 97 + 38 = ?

$$\begin{array}{r} 9\,7 \\ +\ 3\,8 \\ \hline \end{array}$$
So far, so good!
→
$$\begin{array}{r} 1 \\ 9\,7 \\ +\ 3\,8 \\ \hline 5 \end{array}$$

We start by adding the ones column, as usual: 7 + 8 = 15. The 5 stays in the ones column, and the 1 ten goes piggyback in the tens column. So far, so good. Next we add up the tens column: 1 + 9 + 3 = 13. So now we have *13 tens* . . . that means 3 tens and 1 hundred! (Just think back to page 58, where we saw that 10 tens make 1 hundred.) And that means the 1 needs to go in the *hundreds* column.

$$\begin{array}{r} 1\ \ 1 \\ 9\,7 \\ +\ \ 3\,8 \\ \hline 3\,5 \end{array}$$
We've made a new lane!
$$\begin{array}{r} 1\ \ 1 \\ 9\,7 \\ +\ \ 3\,8 \\ \hline 1\,3\,5 \end{array}$$

No problem! So we get 1 hundred, 3 tens, and 5 ones—in other words, **135**. Done!

GAME TIME!

Add these numbers with regrouping. I'll do the first one for you!

1. 436 + 27 = __?__

Let's Play: First, we'll write this as a meowntain (remember our kitties from Chapter 8?) and mark the freeway lanes, making sure everyone stays in their columns. Then we'll add the ones: 6 + 7 = 13. The **3** stays in the ones column, and the **1** rides piggyback on the tens column! Next we add up the tens: 1 + 3 + 2 = 6.

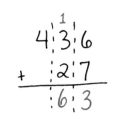 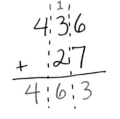 

We still have just 4 hundreds, so that goes in the answer line, too. And that's our total: 4 hundreds, 6 tens, and 3 ones—in other words, 463!
Answer: 436 + 27 = 463

2. 54 + 17 = __?__

3. 28 + 43 = __?__

4. 45 + 39 = __?__

5. 73 + 19 = __?__

6. 65 + 18 = __?__

7. 257 + 34 = __?__

8. 817 + 26 = __?__

9. 98 + 34 = __?__

10. 78 + 56 = __?__

(Answers on page 149.)

"Show All Totals"

There's yet another method of adding with regrouping called "show all totals." In this method, we first add the tens, show that entire total, then add the ones, show that entire total, and then add those two "totals" together to get the final total—the answer! We still want to keep our freeway lanes, though. Here's how the example on page 122 would look:

Step 1

$$9\,|\,7$$
$$+\ \ 3\,|\,8$$

Set it up!

Step 2

$$9\,|\,7$$
$$+\ \ 3\,|\,8$$
$$1\ 2\ 0$$

First add
90 + 30 = 120

BY THE WAY, IT DOESN'T MATTER IF WE START WITH THE ONES OR THE TENS COLUMN FOR THIS METHOD!

Step 3

$$9\,|\,7$$
$$+\ \ 3\,|\,8$$
$$1\ 2\ 0$$
$$1\,|\,5$$

Next add
7 + 8 = 15

Step 4

$$9\,|\,7$$
$$+\ \ 3\,|\,8$$
$$1\ 2\ 0$$
$$+\ \ \ 1\,|\,5$$
$$1\ 3\ 5$$

Then add these!

← Answer!

Notice that with this "show all totals" method, instead of adding 9 + 3, we have to pay attention to the fact that we're actually adding 90 + 30, and then we write the entire 120, being careful to keep everyone in their correct lanes before adding the ones column and then adding them all together.

Even though it's a bit more work, some people prefer this way. **Try the Game Time on page 123 with this method, and see which you like best!**

Beep, Beep! More Lanes! Adding Three-Digit Numbers with Regrouping

In really big cities, they have big freeways—and that means more lanes! And with bigger numbers, everything works the same way as before. . . . There are just more "lanes" to keep track of—more columns! Let's do: 983 + 579. Whoa, this one looks kinda crazy! But we won't crash if we keep all the cars in their correct lanes. And if it makes you happy, remember our pile of kitties. Let's do it!

First, we write it out, with lanes marked:

$$
\begin{array}{r}
\text{hundreds}\,|\,\text{tens}\,|\,\text{ones} \\
9\;\;8\;\;3 \\
+\;5\;\;7\;\;9 \\
\hline
\end{array}
\qquad
\begin{array}{r}
1 \\
9\;\;8\;\;3 \\
+\;5\;\;7\;\;9 \\
\hline
2
\end{array}
\qquad
\begin{array}{r}
1\;\;1 \\
9\;\;8\;\;3 \\
+\;5\;\;7\;\;9 \\
\hline
6\;\;2
\end{array}
$$

Then we add up the ones: 3 + 9 = 12. Great! The 2 stays in the ones column, and the 1 gets to ride piggyback in the tens column. Next we add up the tens: 1 + 8 + 7 = 16. And "16 tens" means we have 6 tens and 1 hundred! So the 6 stays in the tens column and we put the 1 piggyback in the hundreds column. Next we add up the hundreds: 1 + 9 + 5 = 15. Whoa! What do we do now? Well . . . 15 hundreds means we have 5 hundreds and 1 thousand! So we get to create a new thousands lane and put the 1 there.

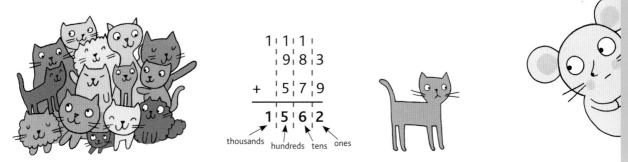

$$
\begin{array}{r}
1\;\;1\;\;1 \\
9\;\;8\;\;3 \\
+\;5\;\;7\;\;9 \\
\hline
1\;\;5\;\;6\;\;2
\end{array}
$$

thousands hundreds tens ones

We get 1 thousand, 5 hundreds, 6 tens, and 2 leftover ones—in other words, 1562. Done!

Answer: 983 + 579 = 1562

GAME TIME!

Add these numbers, using freeways and piggyback rides!

I'll do the first one for you.

1. 501 + 249 = _?_

Let's Play: Don't let the zero scare you off—it actually makes the problem easier! First, we'll put everyone in their lanes. Let's add up the ones lane: 1 + 9 = 10. We ended up with 1 ten and 0 leftover ones! So the 0 stays in the ones place, and we'll put the 1 ten in the tens column.

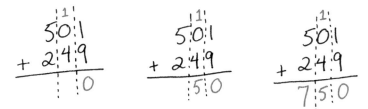

Next, adding the tens, we get: 1 + 0 + 4 = 5, so we have a total of **5** tens, and then we just add up 5 + 2 = **7** for the hundreds column, so our total is **750**. We kept all the cars in their correct lanes, yay!

Answer: 501 + 249 = 750

2. 278 + 173 = _?_   3. 376 + 179 = _?_   4. 802 + 118 = _?_

5. 566 + 256 = _?_   6. 189 + 588 = _?_   7. 743 + 182 = _?_

8. 876 + 345 = _?_   9. 999 + 222 = _?_   10. 828 + 484 = _?_

Great job! We only have one chapter left—can you believe it? We get to learn more about subtraction, and we get to play with googly eyes. . . .

(Answers on page 149.)

Chapter 10

A Big Box of Googly Eyes:
Subtracting with Ungrouping (aka "Borrowing")

Let's say your class is doing an art project with googly eyes. There are a bunch of boxes that have 10 googly eyes each, and it's your job to open the boxes and give some to each of your classmates. In other words, you need to "unbox"  the googly eyes.

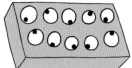

But now there's only one classmate left, and the box you've been using just became empty, so you have to open a *whole new box* just to give her two googly eyes! I mean, there's a stack of boxes next to you, but it's still kind of annoying to have to open a whole new box, right?

Oh well, things like this happen sometimes, even in math! Maybe we should try to be grateful that the boxes are there in the first place. . . .

Unbox Those Googly Eyes: Subtracting Two-Digit Numbers with Ungrouping

Let's do 83 − 64. Just like with addition, we want to keep everyone in their freeway lanes, so let's write it that way:

$$\begin{array}{r} 8\,\vert\,3 \\ -\,6\,\vert\,4 \\ \hline \end{array}$$

Great. So first we look at just the ones column, and we need to subtract: 3 − 4. Wait, what? We can't do that, because 3 isn't big enough to subtract 4 from it . . . but that's okay! After all, we have 8 boxes of googly eyes right next to us—sort of! We have *8 tens* sitting right there. We can take 1 full ten, which is like a box of 10 googly eyes, "open the box," and put the 10 googly eyes in the ones column! This "unboxing" in math is called *ungrouping*. Check it out:

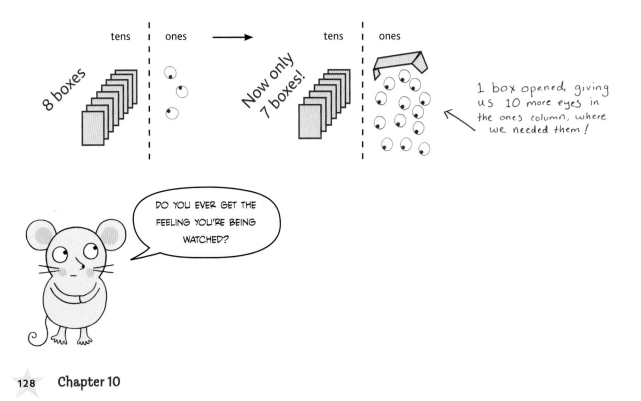

Let's see what this looks like with our numbers! We took 10 from the tens column and gave it to the ones column, right? So the 8 becomes 7 (there are only 7 boxes left) and the 3 becomes 13 (we got 10 new googly eyes from that box)!

And now we have a total of 10 + 3 = **13** ones in the ones column, which is more than enough to do our subtraction in the ones column, yay!

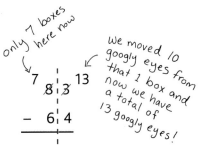

So, for the ones column, we do: 13 − 4 = **9**, and then for the tens column, we do: 7 − 6 = **1**.

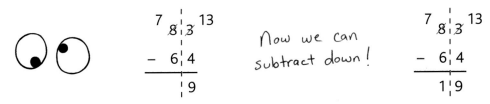

We end up with **1** ten and **9** ones—in other words, **19**! And we've just shown that **83 − 64 = 19**. Nice work!

Two-Digit Subtraction: When Do We Ungroup?

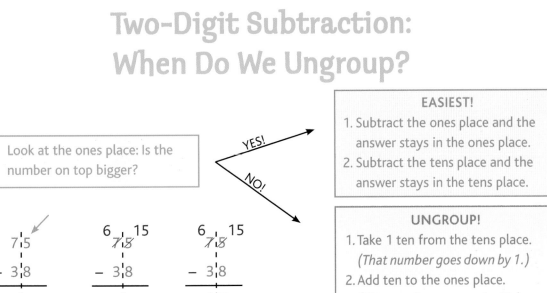

Look at the ones place: Is the number on top bigger?

YES!

NO!

EASIEST!
1. Subtract the ones place and the answer stays in the ones place.
2. Subtract the tens place and the answer stays in the tens place.

UNGROUP!
1. Take 1 ten from the tens place. *(That number goes down by 1.)*
2. Add ten to the ones place. *(That number goes up by 10.)*
3. Subtract the ones.
4. Subtract the tens.

Instead of "ungrouping," some people call this "regrouping" or even "borrowing." But of course it's not really borrowing, because it's not like we're going to ever give those 10 ones back to the tens column.

"NOT REALLY BORROWING." YEP. I HEAR THAT. IT'S LIKE WHEN SOMEONE ASKS TO "BORROW" A TISSUE SO THEY CAN BLOW THEIR NOSE IN IT. BORROW? DO THEY REALLY MEAN "BORROW"?

MR. MOUSE . . . I THINK YOU'RE TRYING TO CHANGE THE SUBJECT.

NO, SERIOUSLY, THEY'RE LIKE, "CAN I BORROW A TISSUE?" AND I'M LIKE, "DON'T BORROW IT--JUST TAKE IT. I DON'T WANT YOUR SNOTTY BOOGERS!"

AREN'T ALL BOOGERS SNOTTY?

MY POINT EXACTLY.

Watch Out!

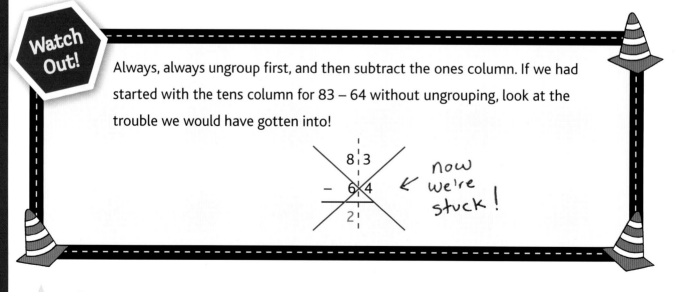

Always, always ungroup first, and then subtract the ones column. If we had started with the tens column for 83 − 64 without ungrouping, look at the trouble we would have gotten into!

← now we're stuck!

Ungrouping with Models!

Remember back in Chapter 5 when we used models for subtraction? We'd first model the bigger number, and then cross off the parts we're subtracting. For example, on pages 73 and 74, for 86 − 34, first we modeled 86, then crossed off 34 and circled what was left over: 52!

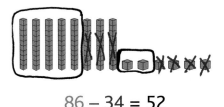

$$86 - 34 = 52$$

Now let's subtract 56 − 39. Okay, first we'll model 56 with 5 tens and 6 ones, right? Next we want to cross off 39, but wait—there aren't 9 ones to cross off, are there? I guess it's time to open a box of googly eyes—I mean, *ungroup* one of those ten sticks into 10 little ones!

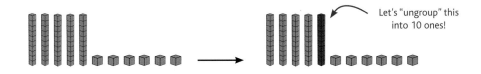

Let's "ungroup" this into 10 ones!

Here's what it looks like when we "ungroup" the ten, and now we're ready to cross stuff off.

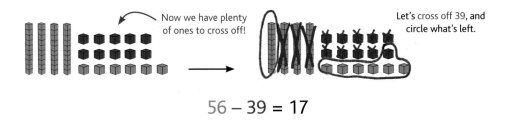

Now we have plenty of ones to cross off!

Let's cross off 39, and circle what's left.

$$56 - 39 = 17$$

We just showed with models that 56 − 39 = **17**! Ta-da!

Choices!

When you do these subtraction problems with ungrouping, you can choose to think about (and draw!) the models like we just did, or think about boxes of googly eyes, or not! You can also simply draw the freeway lanes and make the numbers change. It's your brain—so do what you like most!

PUT YOUR THINKING CAP ON!

Whenever things feel extra challenging, remember to put your thinking cap on, like we talked about on page 39. You got this!

It's nice to have choices, don't you think? But no matter how we choose to think about ungrouping, it's very important to *check our answers*, because it's so easy to make mistakes along the way, especially with subtraction!

Return of the Turkey Sandwich: Checking Our Answers with Addition!

Remember the "turkey sandwich" fact families we talked about in Chapter 2? Well, every time we do *any* addition or subtraction problem, we are discovering a new turkey sandwich—a new fact family! And because of that, <u>we can use addition to check our subtraction answers.</u>

turkey + bread = sandwich	bread + turkey = sandwich
sandwich – turkey = bread	sandwich – bread = turkey

On page 128 we did the subtraction problem 83 – 64 = 19, which is like destroying the sandwich, remember? And the "sandwich" is the biggest number: 83! So if we *made* the sandwich, we could do: 64 + 19 = 83 or 19 + 64 = 83—it doesn't matter which we choose. Let's try it:

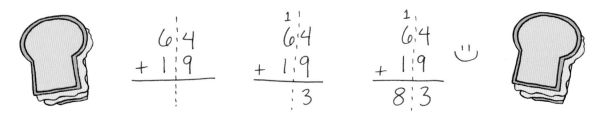

Yep, we got 83! Since making and destroying turkey sandwiches is all part of the same fact family (shown below in a box), we know we did our subtraction problem correctly. Yay!

GAME TIME!

Do these subtraction problems using ungrouping, and then do an addition problem to check your answer. I'll do the first one for you!

1. 40 − 28 = __?__

Let's Play: Okay, first we'll stack these up and draw the freeway lanes. Next we'd love to subtract 0 − 8, but we can't! Let's fix this by grabbing a ten from the tens column, so we're left with 3 tens there, and we'll add our new ten to the **ones** column. There was just a 0 in the ones column before, and now it becomes 10!

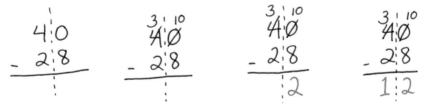

Next we subtract—making sure to start with the ones column: 10 − 8 = **2**, and then the tens column: 3 − 2 = **1**. So we're left with **1** ten and **2** ones, in other words, **12**! There's our answer! Let's <u>check our work</u>, by putting the turkey sandwich back together like this: 28 + 12, and hope we get 40:

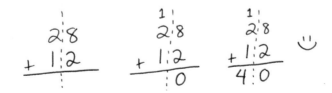

Great, the turkey sandwich works, so we got the subtraction problem right!

Answer: 40 − 28 = 12

Keep going! ⟶

2. 82 − 24 = ?

3. 61 − 36 = ?

4. 77 − 29 = ?

5. 92 − 18 = ?

6. 30 − 17 = ?

7. 91 − 19 = ?

8. 87 − 78 = ?

9. 34 − 18 = ?

10. 61 − 23 = ?

EVEN THOUGH I DIDN'T WANT TO CHECK MY ANSWERS WITH ADDITION, IT'S A GREAT FEELING WHEN IT ACTUALLY WORKS!

(Answers on page 149.)

Back on the Big Freeway—with Googly Eyes: Subtracting Three-Digit Numbers with Ungrouping!

They say you should never drive when you're angry because it makes you an unsafe driver. They never said we couldn't drive with googly eyes. . . .

Let's do 862 − 479. No problem! First we'll draw our freeway lanes. Then we start like we always do—with the ones column!

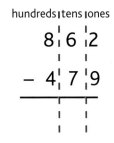

```
hundreds  tens  ones
    8  |  6  |  2
  − 4  |  7  |  9
    ¦     ¦
```

In the ones column, since we can't subtract 2 − 9, <u>we'll take 1 ten</u> from the tens column. So that means we change the 6 to a 5, and now we have 12 ones—plenty to subtract with. Now we're ready to subtract the ones column, and we get 12 − 9 = **3**. So far, so good? Great!

We take 1 ten and get 10 ones!

```
  ı 5 ı 12
  8ı 6 ı2
   ı   ı
 − 4ı 7 ı9
  ———————
   ı   ı
```

Now we can subtract the ones!

```
  ı 5 ı 12
  8ı 6 ı2
   ı   ı
 − 4ı 7 ı9
  ———————
   ı   ı3
```

But what now? I mean, we can't subtract 5 − 7! We don't have enough tens! Well, I've heard that there are big packages that hold 10 *boxes* of googly eyes—and we know the boxes have 10 eyes each, so that's 100 googly eyes total! Yep, we're going to <u>take 1 hundred</u> from the hundreds column in order to get 10 tens!

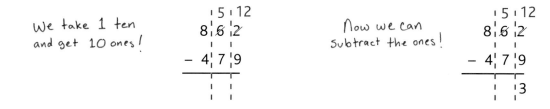

GOES DOWN BY ONE   GOES UP BY TEN

THIS WORKS BECAUSE 1 HUNDRED = 10 TENS.

```
        15
  7 ı 5 ı 12
  8ı 6 ı2
   ı   ı
 − 4ı 7 ı9
  ———————
   ı   ı3
```

This means we need to cross out the 8 from the hundreds column and make it a **7** . . . and then we need to change the 5 to a **15** in the tens column! Crazy, right? But it works!

Now we can finish subtracting down!

```
            15
      7 ı 5 ı 12
      8ı 6 ı2
       ı   ı
     − 4ı 7 ı9
      ———————
      3ı 8 ı3
       ı   ı
```

Next we subtract the tens column: 15 − 7 = 8, and then the hundreds column is 7 − 4 = 3. We're left with **3** hundreds, **8** tens, and **3** ones—in other words, **383**! Done! Well, sort of . . .

We've just shown that **862 − 479 = 383**. But it sure seems like we could have made a mistake somewhere in there, doesn't it? Let's check our answer by making a turkey sandwich. (See page 134 if you have no idea what I'm talking about.) So let's try 479 + 383 and hope we get 862!

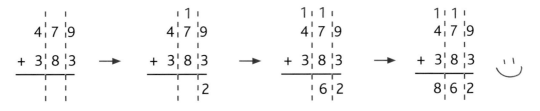

Great! That means we got the right answer. Done!

Answer: 862 − 479 = 383

I LIKE HOW IT FEELS IN MY BRAIN WHEN I GET A PROBLEM RIGHT.

Your brain is getting stronger, one math problem at a time!

LET'S PRACTICE!

GAME TIME!

Subtract these bigger numbers using ungrouping, and then check your answer with an addition problem. I'll do the first one for you!

1. 9407 − 692 = ?

Let's Play: We'll stack the numbers and draw freeway lanes, and look, the ones column is easy: 7 − 2 = 5. Great! In the tens column, we can't do 0 − 9, so we'll ungroup one hundred (changing 4 to 3) to get 10 tens (changing 0 to 10). Now we can subtract the tens column: 10 − 9 = 1.

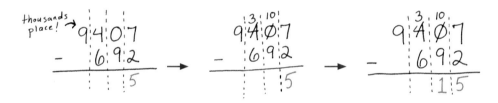

In the hundreds column, we can't do 3 − 6, right? So let's ungroup 1 thousand (changing 9 to 8) to get 10 new hundreds (changing 3 to 13). Now we can subtract 13 − 6 = 7!

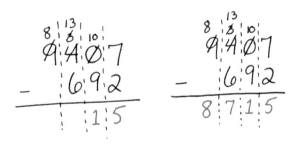

And there's nothing to subtract in the thousands column, so we can just write the **8** down below. We're left with **8** thousands, **7** hundreds, **1** ten, and **5** ones—in other words, **8715**. Phew!

We've shown that 9407 − 692 = 8715, but now let's **check our work** by putting the turkey sandwich back together—we'll add 8715 + 692 and hope we get 9407. If we do, that means we did the subtraction right!

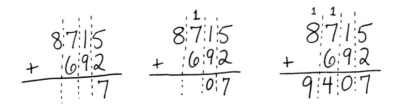

Yep, looks good!

Answer: 9407 − 692 = 8715

2. 457 − 294 = ?

3. 777 − 168 = ?

4. 868 − 686 = ?

5. 853 − 362 = ?

6. 345 − 181 = ?

7. 957 − 167 = ?

8. 908 − 457 = ?

9. 653 − 79 = ?

10. 121 − 78 = ?

Great job!

(Answers on page 149.)

Before we finish the chapter, I want to show you what happens when we have to ungroup <u>twice</u> before even starting to subtract! First, picture this: let's say we need 87 googly eyes, but there aren't any individual boxes left—just 5 packages to open. Let's do 500 − 87.

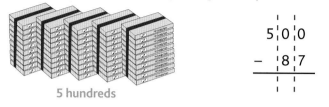

5 hundreds

For the ones column, we can't subtract 0 − 7, right? So we try to take 1 ten from the tens column—but wait, there's only a 0—there are no tens to take! That means we have to take 1 *hundred* so the 5 becomes a 4, and then that <u>1 hundred</u> becomes <u>10 tens</u> in the *tens* column. Yep, now we have 4 hundreds packages and 10 individual boxes.

4 hundreds   10 tens

Hmm, but we still have to open one of those *boxes* to get to the googly eyes, right? So we have to ungroup *again*—this time in the tens column. So we open a box to get 10 ones, and this turns the 10 into a 9, and in the ones column, the 0 becomes 10. Finally, some ones!

4 hundreds   9 tens   10 ones

I told you it was crazy—just look at all that opening of googly eye boxes, and the subtraction hasn't even happened yet! Now we can subtract—starting with the ones column, as always:

9
4 10 10
5̶ 0̶ 0̶
−   8 7
━━━━━
    3

→

9
4 10 10
5̶ 0̶ 0̶
−   8 7
━━━━━
  1 3

→

9
4 10 10
5̶ 0̶ 0̶
−   8 7
━━━━━
4 1 3

And that's ← our answer!

So we got **500 – 87 = 413**. And of course, we can check our answer by adding 413 + 87 and hoping we get 500:

$$\begin{array}{r} 4\,1\,3 \\ +\ \ 8\,7 \\ \hline \end{array} \qquad \begin{array}{r} {}^{1} \\ 4\,1\,3 \\ +\ \ 8\,7 \\ \hline 0 \end{array} \qquad \begin{array}{r} {}^{1\,1} \\ 4\,1\,3 \\ +\ \ 8\,7 \\ \hline 0\,0 \end{array} \qquad \begin{array}{r} {}^{1\,1} \\ 4\,1\,3 \\ +\ \ 8\,7 \\ \hline 5\,0\,0 \end{array} \quad yay!$$

Great, we did it!

Do Not Read These Acknowledgments

Thank you to my parents, Mahaila and Chris, for always encouraging and believing in me! Thank you to my best friend in the whole world, Crystal, and to her husband, Mike, and their darling children, Cricket and little Cayden, whose birth I witnessed just two hours after writing part of Chapter 9 of this book! Thank you to the rest of my wonderful family, including but not limited to Chris Jr., Connor, Lorna (and kids!), Molly, the Svesloskys, Sims, and Vertas. And to Grammy (1910–2010) and Opa (1919–2016), who were always so proud of me, and whose voicemails are still saved on my phone to prove it. Thank you, Cheryl, for all your help to our family in so many ways, and thank you, Kim, for just everything! A huge thank-you to Mike Verta for being a great co-parenting partner, and for another phenomenal title and cover.

Thank you to my wonderful illustrator, Maranda Maberry, for bringing my characters to life. Thank you to everyone at PRH, including Phoebe Yeh and the incomparable Barbara Marcus, for your vision and belief in me. Thank you to my talented (and tireless!) editor Emily Easton. I'm so grateful for your partnership on all of our books together, but especially this one! (And for putting up with all my exclamation points!) Thank you to Elizabeth Tardiff, Nicole de las Heras, and Monique Razzouk for all the involved design work in this book, and Alison Kolani, Megan Williams, Samantha Gentry, Amy Bowman, and more, for bringing it all together. All your hard work is so very appreciated. These books are more complex than most realize, and it takes a village.

Thank you to my longtime literary agent, Laura Nolan, for first seeking me out over ten years ago to start writing books to inspire kids in math, and for encouraging me to continue with a younger crowd. Thank you to my literary lawyer, Stephen Breimer, and also to Cathey Lizzio, Pat Brady, and Matt Sherman for your many years of support, and thank you to Michelle Bega at Rogers & Cowan, Mary McCue, and Noreen Herits for helping me get the word out about my books. Thank you to all my friends at Hallmark Channel, including Bill Abbott, Michelle Vicary, and Randy Pope, for working my movies around my crazy book schedule! Thank you to everyone who proofread this book, including my mom, Mahaila McKellar; Mike Scafati; Damon Williams; Mariko Garcia; Ann Shimizu; Joanna Fay; and the outstandingly astute Jonathan Farley. Thank you to the educators who read my very first draft many moons ago and gave feedback, including Laura Chambless, Nancy Frantz, Sue Descher, Mariko Garcia, and Kelsie Provost. Thank you to Dan Degrow for your unwavering support, and also to Tami Cronce, Crista Woolum, and Betsy Shuman and more for giving me insights into today's classroom experience.

Thank you to my amazing, loving husband, Scott—I love you so much and feel so lucky to be married to you. Thank you to Hunter for being a wonderful teenage stepson (and awesome football player), and for even letting me help you with math sometimes. Finally, thank you to my precious boy, Draco. You have changed me forever, in the best ways possible, and it is my greatest honor to watch you grow and help you thrive. I love you!

Chapter 1

p. 15:   2. 5 + 5 = 10   3. 7 + 3 = 10   4. 6 + 4 = 10   5. 3 + 7 = 10

p. 17:   2. We'd walk up 7 steps. 3 + 7 = 10   3. We'd walk up 1 step. 9 + 1 = 10
4. We'd walk up 5 steps. 5 + 5 = 10   5. We'd walk up 3 steps. 7 + 3 = 10

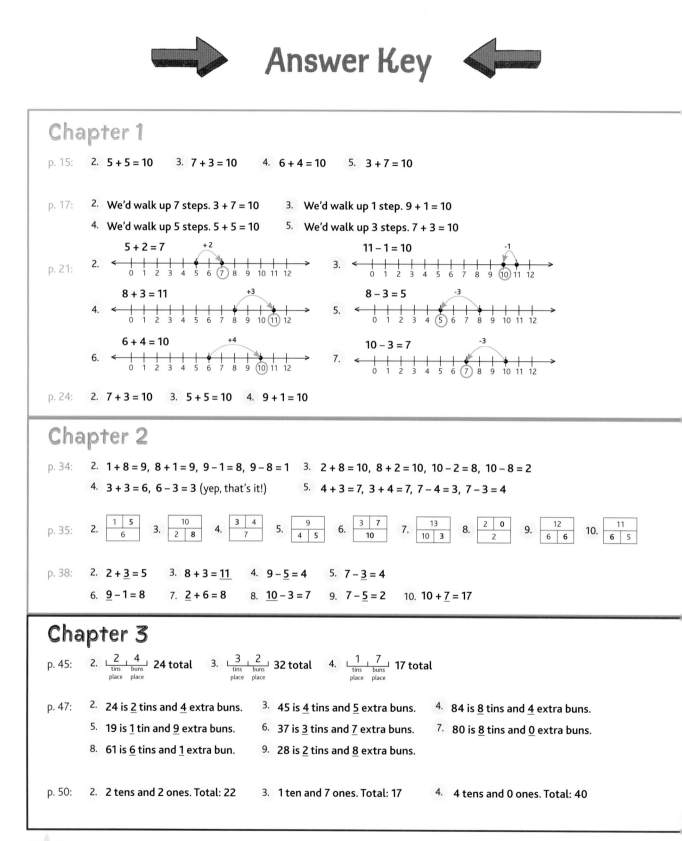

p. 21:   2. 5 + 2 = 7   3. 11 − 1 = 10
4. 8 + 3 = 11   5. 8 − 3 = 5
6. 6 + 4 = 10   7. 10 − 3 = 7

p. 24:   2. 7 + 3 = 10   3. 5 + 5 = 10   4. 9 + 1 = 10

Chapter 2

p. 34:   2. 1 + 8 = 9, 8 + 1 = 9, 9 − 1 = 8, 9 − 8 = 1   3. 2 + 8 = 10, 8 + 2 = 10, 10 − 2 = 8, 10 − 8 = 2
4. 3 + 3 = 6, 6 − 3 = 3 (yep, that's it!)   5. 4 + 3 = 7, 3 + 4 = 7, 7 − 4 = 3, 7 − 3 = 4

p. 35:   2. | 1 | 5 |
         | 6 |

3. | 10 |
    | 2 | 8 |

4. | 3 | 4 |
    | 7 |

5. | 9 |
    | 4 | 5 |

6. | 3 | 7 |
    | 10 |

7. | 13 |
    | 10 | 3 |

8. | 2 | 0 |
    | 2 |

9. | 12 |
    | 6 | 6 |

10. | 11 |
     | 6 | 5 |

p. 38:   2. 2 + 3 = 5   3. 8 + 3 = 11   4. 9 − 5 = 4   5. 7 − 3 = 4
6. 9 − 1 = 8   7. 2 + 6 = 8   8. 10 − 3 = 7   9. 7 − 5 = 2   10. 10 + 7 = 17

Chapter 3

p. 45:   2. 2 | 4   24 total
             tins | buns
             place   place

3. 3 | 2   32 total
    tins | buns
    place   place

4. 1 | 7   17 total
    tins | buns
    place   place

p. 47:   2. 24 is 2 tins and 4 extra buns.   3. 45 is 4 tins and 5 extra buns.   4. 84 is 8 tins and 4 extra buns.
5. 19 is 1 tin and 9 extra buns.   6. 37 is 3 tins and 7 extra buns.   7. 80 is 8 tins and 0 extra buns.
8. 61 is 6 tins and 1 extra bun.   9. 28 is 2 tins and 8 extra buns.

p. 50:   2. 2 tens and 2 ones. Total: 22   3. 1 ten and 7 ones. Total: 17   4. 4 tens and 0 ones. Total: 40

2. 36 is 3 tens and 6 ones.   3. 63 is 6 tens and 3 ones.   4. 59 is 5 tens and 9 ones.   5. 12 is 1 ten and 2 ones.

6. The 5 in 45 stands for 5 birds.   7. The 8 in 82 stands for 80 hippopotamuses.

8. The 8 in 58 stands for 8 monkeys.   9. The 5 in 50 stands for 50 cubs.

p. 54:   2. 2 dimes and 1 penny   3. 3 dimes and 4 pennies   4. 4 dimes and 5 pennies   5. 6 dimes and 7 pennies

6. 5 dimes and 0 pennies   7. 1 dime and 8 pennies

Chapter 4

p. 60:   2. 346 total buns   3. 171 total buns   4. 203 total buns

p. 62:   2. "Two hundred ninety gray kittens." The 9 stands for 90 kittens.   3. "Eight hundred forty-three white mice." The 8 stands for 800 mice.   4. "One hundred fifty-eight pink ponies." The 8 stands for 8 ponies.

5. "Six hundred seventy-two yellow giraffes." The 7 stands for 70 giraffes.

p. 64:   2. 9, and it stands for 9.   3. 3, and it stands for 300.   4. 5, and it stands for 50.   5. 8, and it stands for 800.

6. 8, and it stands for 80.   7. 0, and it stands for 0.   8. 9, and it stands for 9.   9. 6, and it stands for 600.

p. 66:   2. 5 dollars, 2 dimes, and 4 pennies   3. 8 dollars, 6 dimes, and 7 pennies

4. 2 dollars and 1 penny (no dimes)   5. 9 dollars and 8 dimes (no pennies)

Chapter 5

p. 71:   2. $12 + 33 = 45$ 3. $24 + 22 = 46$ 4. $40 + 50 = 90$ 5. $31 + 21 = 52$

p. 75:   2. $43 - 11 = 32$, so 32 buns are left.   3. $71 - 20 = 51$, so 51 buns are left.

4. $26 - 13 = 13$, so 13 buns are left.   5. $38 - 17 = 21$, so 21 buns are left.

p. 76:   2. $153 + 410 = \underline{563}$ 3. $343 + 55 = \underline{398}$

4. $323 - 201 = \underline{122}$ 5. $135 - 120 = \underline{15}$

Chapter 6

p. 81:   2. $10 + 5 = 15$, which means $9 + 6 = 15$ 3. $10 + 2 = 12$, which means $7 + 5 = 12$

4. $10 + 6 = 16$, which means $9 + 7 = 16$ 5. $10 + 3 = 13$, which means $8 + 5 = 13$

6. $1 + 10 = 11$, which means $3 + 8 = 11$ 7. $10 + 2 = 12$, which means $6 + 6 = 12$

p. 83:   2. $12 - 3 = 9$ 3. $14 - 5 = 9$ 4. $12 - 7 = 5$ 5. $14 - 6 = 8$ 6. $15 - 8 = 7$ 7. $17 - 8 = 9$

8. $16 - 9 = 7$ 9. $18 - 9 = 9$

p. 87:   2. $68 + 10 = 78$ 3. $86 - 10 = 76$ 4. $45 + 10 = 55$ 5. $76 + 10 = 86$ 6. $87 - 10 = 77$

7. $24 - 10 = 14$ 8. $16 + 10 = 26$ 9. $59 - 10 = 49$ 10. $91 - 10 = 81$ 11. $33 - 10 = 23$

p. 88:   2. $45 + 20 = 65$ 3. $98 - 30 = 68$ 4. $34 + 10 = 44$ 5. $78 - 40 = 38$ 6. $29 + 70 = 99$

7. $41 + 50 = 91$ 8. $56 + 40 = 96$ 9. $66 - 60 = 6$

Chapter 7

p. 91:   2. $9 + 5$ is the same as $10 + 4$ 3. $8 + 5$ is the same as $10 + 3$ 4. $9 + 7$ is the same as $10 + 6$

5. $9 + 9$ is the same as $10 + 8$ 6. $3 + 8$ is the same as $10 + 1$ 7. $6 + 7$ is the same as $10 + 3$

8. $8 + 7$ is the same as $10 + 5$ 9. $9 + 8$ is the same as $10 + 7$ 10. $6 + 5$ is the same as $10 + 1$

11. $6 + 9$ is the same as $10 + 5$

p. 94:   2. $10 + 4 = 14$, which means $9 + 5 = 14$ 3. $10 + 5 = 15$, which means $9 + 6 = 15$

4. $10 + 5 = 15$, which means $8 + 7 = 15$ 5. $15 + 10 = 25$, which means $17 + 8 = 25$

6. $6 + 20 = 26$, which means $8 + 18 = 26$ 7. $10 + 1 = 11$, which means $7 + 4 = 11$

8. $2 + 20 = 22$ or $10 + 12 = 22$, which means $6 + 16 = 22$ 9. $10 + 8 = 18$ or $8 + 10 = 18$, which means $9 + 9 = 18$

10. $10 + 3 = 13$, which means $7 + 6 = 13$ 11. $11 + 10 = 21$, which means $15 + 6 = 21$

p. 99:   2. $65 + 11 = 76$ 3. $22 + 38 = 60$

4. $33 + 9 = 42$ 5. $19 + 13 = 32$

6. $16 + 68 = 84$ 7. $84 + 7 = 91$

8. $59 + 13 = 72$ 9. $28 + 13 = 41$

10. $12 + 47 = 59$

Chapter 8

p. 103:   2. $186 = 100 + 80 + 6$ 3. $324 = 300 + 20 + 4$ 4. $59 = 50 + 9$ 5. $425 = 400 + 20 + 5$

6. $99 = 90 + 9$ 7. $311 = 300 + 10 + 1$ 8. $888 = 800 + 80 + 8$ 9. $567 = 500 + 60 + 7$

10. $717 = 700 + 10 + 7$ 11. $950 = 900 + 50$ 12. $12 = 10 + 2$ 13. $501 = 500 + 1$

p. 105:   2. $500 + 90 + 8 = 598$ 3. $700 + 40 + 6 = 746$ 4. $100 + 10 + 1 = 111$ 5. $600 + 10 + 9 = 619$

6. $100 + 20 + 3 = 123$ 7. $900 + 80 + 7 = 987$ 8. $90 + 9 = 99$ 9. $900 + 30 = 930$

10. $800 + 8 = 808$

Chapter 9

Chapter 10

Index

"New Math" Translation Guide—for Grown-Ups!

Here's a guide to some newer math terms and methods, and where to find out more about them in the book.

Fact Family (p. 31) <u>A group of addition and subtraction facts</u> that use the same (usually three) numbers; for example, 4, 6, and 10. *Fact families* show kids that addition and subtraction facts are "related" to each other. It also shows why we can check our subtraction problems with addition (p. 134).

$$6 + 4 = 10 \qquad 10 = 6 + 4$$
$$4 + 6 = 10 \qquad 10 = 4 + 6$$
$$10 - 6 = 4 \qquad 4 = 10 - 6$$
$$10 - 4 = 6 \qquad 6 = 10 - 4$$

Models (p. 68) <u>Pictures to show numbers</u>—usually ones, tens, and hundreds. These can be useful for "seeing" *place value* and for adding and subtracting bigger numbers (pp. 74, 121, 131). Here's what 123 looks like as a model:

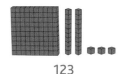

123

Number Bonds (p. 25) These are diagrams often used to show a math sentence (for example, 4 + 6 = 10), and they are also a short way to write an entire *fact family*.

Part-Part-Whole Box (p. 32) <u>A picture that uses three numbers to show a *fact family*.</u> This is another short way to write a fact family.

Regrouping (p. 119) Regrouping = *carrying*. This is when we're adding, we get more than 10 in a column, and we have to put a little 1 in the column to the left (in two-digit addition, this *groups* 10 little ones into 1 ten). Check out the example on p. 121 for more! Another term sometimes used: *trading*. (Some people even use *regrouping* to mean both *carrying* in addition <u>and</u> *borrowing* in subtraction.)

$$\begin{array}{r} 1 \\ 5\,9 \\ +\ 3\,6 \\ \hline 9\,5 \end{array}$$

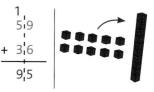

Ten Frame (p. 23) <u>A 2 x 5 rectangle with 10 spots.</u> Ten frames help kids "see" ten. Using two different objects, this ten frame shows the math sentence 7 + 3 = 10. Ten frames are also useful in mental math for addition and subtraction. (See Chapter 6!)

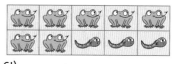

Ungrouping (p. 127) Ungrouping = *borrowing*. This is when we're subtracting and we have to take value from the column *to the left* in order to keep going (in two-digit subtraction, this *ungroups* 1 ten into 10 little ones). Check out the example on p. 131 for more! Other terms sometimes used: *regrouping, decomposing*.

$$\begin{array}{r} 6\ \ 15 \\ 7\,8 \\ -\ 3\,8 \\ \hline 3\,7 \end{array}$$

Danica McKellar is the *New York Times* bestselling author of groundbreaking math books including the board book *Bathtime Mathtime*, picture books *Goodnight, Numbers* and *Ten Magic Butterflies*, and the middle school hit *Kiss My Math*, and is a summa cum laude graduate of UCLA with a degree in mathematics. She is also well known for her acting roles on *The Wonder Years*, *The West Wing*, multiple Hallmark Channel movies, and more. Visit McKellarMath.com to see the ever-growing line of Danica's helpful, fun math books!